TWENTY REMARKABLE WOMEN

SEEN THROUGH THEIR HANDWRITING

TWENTY REMARKABLE WOMEN

SEEN THROUGH

THEIR HANDWRITING

For Betty — Enjoy
Marian Brannan '05

MARIAN GIMBY BRANNAN

LITTLE RIVER PRESS

LITTLE RIVER, CALIFORNIA

LITTLE RIVER PRESS
Post Office Box 507
Little River, California 95456

Copyright © 2004 Marian Gimby Brannan

All Rights Reserved. No part of this book may be reprinted in any manner
without written permission from Little River Press, with the exception of brief
quotations for book reviews.

TEXT & COVER DESIGN: COLORED HORSE STUDIOS
AUTHOR PHOTO ON BACK COVER: LANCE BROWN

FIRST EDITION

Twenty Remarkable Women: Seen Through Their Handwriting
by Marian Gimby Brannan

For book orders, contact your favorite bookstore or via links at
www.mariangimbybrannan.com

ISBN, PAPERBACK EDITION: 1-59457-144-9
ISBN, HARDCOVER EDITION: 1-59457-706-4

TABLE OF CONTENTS

TO MY READER

The journey, the evolvement and, finally, the coming to life of this book has been an incredible experience.

Early on, as I attempted to put myself in the place of the reader, a connection became apparent. Of particular importance to me was the hope that, as you read, you will find that character and personality can indeed be deduced from handwriting.

Graphoanalysis is a simple, accessible tool which, with study and application, makes it possible to understand ourselves and those around us. It has been said that we are three persons: The person *we* think we are, the person *other people* think we are and the person we *really* are. The examination of handwriting and what it may reveal is one way of finding out who we *really* are.

Twenty Remarkable Women is the launching pad from which you, the reader, can come to know these women more intimately. While doing this, you may find some of the intimacies of your own personality.

HAPPY READING!

A REFLECTION ON WOMEN
Their Essence—Their Uniqueness

WE HAVE TAKEN this opportunity, 2000 years since the birth of Christ, to acknowledge women of the second millennium: their achievements and their contributions to society during this time. This has been done by looking at women as history has recorded their lives and, from a purely human aspect, by examining and analyzing the unique traits and dominant themes of their handwriting.

Handwritten papers, especially in the early centuries of the millennium, were not always available. Wars, revolutions, plagues and the ravages of time had a devastating effect on the preservation of manuscripts, letters and agreements. There was a scarcity of the handwritten word. The handwriting of women with only a few exceptions, was even scarcer, since most women at that time in history had not been taught to write. Those who were educated usually had their thoughts written by scribes, making it difficult to find the known writing of women of antiquity. The earliest valid sample of handwriting, available to us, was a copy of the signature of Joan of Arc, dated 1429.

In our research of women we became aware of the unique and exceptional makeup of a woman, past and present. She is a mother—a daughter—a wife—a single woman. However, her intrinsic nature is one of the homemaker, the teacher, the builder of the nest and the protector of the hearth.

Sadly to say, the history of women is that, although women cherished culture and art, they were not recognized, nor were they given credit for their intellectual contributions. Very little of women's achievements can be found in history.

The obstacles, which continue to be put before women in many parts of the world, have kept them from being fully integrated into social, political and economic life. The dignity of women has often been unacknowledged, and their prerogatives misrepresented.

Woman has been the trustee of humanity, for she bears its children. It is she who teaches children to be civilized, to be human. She transmits faith and culture and makes it possible for our society to continue. In times of necessity she finds, within herself, an inner strength, an innate quality to protect and a God-given quality to carry on. These are her greatest gifts: her essence and her uniqueness. It is no surprise that a woman is seen holding the balancing scales of Justice and that, in Holy Scripture, Wisdom is referred to in the feminine.

We have designated certain women in this book as being remarkable. This is not to say that we are unaware of the many thousands of women who are remarkable in their own right. The media does not mention them, but they are there, often working under extreme difficulties: the mother, the daughter, the wife and the single woman.

HISTORY OF HANDWRITING ANALYSIS
From Antiquity to the Standardized Study of Graphoanalysis

IN SOME INSTITUTES of higher learning, graphology is part of the curriculum. In Europe, perhaps the most famous diploma in Graphology is offered by the Societé Francais de Graphologie in Paris, established in 1901. There is evidence that Graphology is offered at degree level in two Universities in Italy: Urbino and Lumsa (Rome). In 2003 Urbino offered a Master's Degree in Graphology. In 1997 the Ministry of Education of Argentina formally recognized a degree in graphology. It is being taught at Emerson University in Buenos Aires.

Interest in handwriting, as an indicator of character and personality, appears to have existed as far back as Aesop, legendary composer of Greek fables in the Sixth Century B.C., and Aristotle, in the Fourth Century B.C., both of whom were exponents of the art. Two thousand years ago comments were written concerning the relationship of handwriting of various Roman Emperors to their character. In the Eleventh Century A.D., Chinese philosopher and painter, Kuo Jo-Hsu, of the Sung Dynasty, documented observations of his study of handwriting.

The first systematic attempts to relate handwriting with character were made in Italy at the beginning of the Seventeenth Century, by Alderisius Prosper and court physician, Camillo Baldo.

Graphology, as a systematic study, has had a limited history. The term, itself, was unknown until 1871. Abbe Michon, and his teacher, Abbe Flandrin, began the French school of handwriting analysis, calling it Graphology. They used what they referred to as *definite signs,* in evaluating handwriting, and devoted their lives to the study. Later, J. Crepieux-Jamin broke away from those limiting handwriting *signs* and approached the study from a more *gestalt* or overall viewpoint. Further research was done by the famous French psychologist, Alfred Binet (father of the intelligence test), and the psychiatrist, Rogues de Fursac. Many other physicians and psychologists in France have carried on the study. In the early Twentieth Century,

Dr. Albert Schweitzer was a member of the Honorary Committee of the Societé de Graphologie de Paris.

Late in the Nineteenth Century, German scientists assumed leadership. In 1895, Wilheim Preyer, professor of physiology at the University of Jena, suggested that writing originates in the brain, not in the fingers; that handwriting is actually *brain writing.*

Other prominent men and women of the Nineteenth Century were intrigued by handwriting analysis. Among them were George Sands, Honoré de Balzac, Robert Browning and his wife, Elizabeth Barrett, Guy de Maupassant, Benjamin Disraeli, Alexander Dumas, Sir Walter Scott, Sir Arthur Conan Doyle and Edgar Allen Poe.

Neurologist Rudolf Pophal, professor emeritus of graphology at the University of Hamburg, furthered the systematic study, as did the brilliant Georg Meyer. Germany's most authoritative proponent was the philosopher, Ludwig Klages, whose book, *Handwriting and Character,* was written in 1917.

In Austria, in the early thirties, graphologists, Rafael Schermann and Roda Wieser, contributed further research. The outstanding proponent of Graphology, in Switzerland, was Dr. Max Pulver, a psychologist at the University of Zurich who, in 1934, identified three zones in handwriting. In England, Robert Saudek, Hans Jacoby and J. Eysenck produced further material regarding the validity of handwriting analysis.

The roots of handwriting analysis in America go back to 1910, when M.N. Bunker began what was to become years of private study and research, focusing on the strokes of handwriting. He also studied handwriting analysis theories developed by European scholars. His study and research resulted in the founding of the International Graphoanalysis Society in 1949. IGAS has become a respected discipline with a Code of Ethics. It is recognized as a standardized method of analyzing handwriting.

GRAPHOANALYSIS

Graphoanalysis is the study of individual strokes of handwriting. It identifies the character and personality of the writer, regardless of his or her age, sex or nationality. It is not occult, nor is it related, in any way, to pseudoscientific approaches. It is a standardized method of personality assessment, based on research conducted over the past ninety plus years. Graphoanalysis is being further validated by statistical studies, both within the framework of institutions of higher learning and in private research.

Further information about Graphoanalysis may be found by contacting the International Graphoanalysis Society at: www.igas.com.

Marian Gimby Brannan

Marian Gimby Brannan, Master Graphoanalyst

THE READER OF this book should bear in mind that no reproduction of handwriting can fully convey the emotional quality and vitality of the original script.

The analyses and themes on handwriting in this book have been written without bias or judgment, based on my interpretation of the writing of each woman. Each conclusion is in accordance with my training as a Master Graphoanalyst, a member in good standing of the International Graphoanalysis Society, for the past thirty-nine years.

DEDICATION

To my husband Bill whose honesty, integrity and passion for life have profoundly affected me, and whose love and constant encouragement made the completion of this book possible.

To our seven wonderful children and their loved ones who have filled my life until *my cup runneth over*.

To my mother, Elsie, my sister, Jean, and all the other courageous women in my life who have inspired me to write this book.

Last but not least, to my father, Albert, and my brothers, Bobby and Gerry, whose memories I cherish.

CHAPTER 1

MARIAN ANDERSON

1902-1993

Handwriting points the way from me to you.

DR. ALFRED ADLER,

AUSTRIAN PSYCHIATRIST, 1870–1937

"AT AGE TEN I heard, for the first time, the singing of Marian Anderson on a record. I listened, thinking, 'This can't be just a voice, so rich and beautiful.' It was a revelation. And I wept." Jessye Norman, soprano.

Marian Anderson is justly considered to be one of the outstanding vocal talents of the Twentieth Century. With a wide-ranging contralto voice, the centerpiece of her concerts and recordings, was the Negro spiritual. However, she also excelled in operatic arias and is best remembered by her deep-toned voice, when she sang Franz Schubert's *Ave Maria.* The combination of her powerful voice and the stateliness of her stage presence—closed eyes and minimal gestures—electrified audiences around the world.

Marian's autobiography, *Lord What a Morning,* tells of a stable childhood in Philadelphia. She fondly recalls the family's well-planned outings. Lunches were packed and snacks prepared for the annual trip on the trolley train to see the Barnum and Bailey Circus. The family would return tired and happy at the day's end.

The biggest day of the year, however, was Easter. Marian and her two sisters wore new bonnets covered with bright ribbons and flowers. Her father worked at odd jobs to help pay for those bonnets. Marian was enrolled in the church junior choir at age six, where she and a friend sang a duet; her first public appearance. When hearing music and songs in an adjoining room at school, it was as though Marian's whole being was transplanted into that other room; the music would fill her soul. You can imagine her joy when she finally was allowed to join the singing group.

Marian's mother, a former teacher in Lynchville, Virginia, instilled in her children the importance of completing their studies. "If it takes you half an hour to do your lessons, and it takes someone else fifteen minutes, take the half-hour and do them right" was a dictum Marian remembered well.

The Anderson children would find ways to earn money: five cents for scrubbing the neighbor's stairs and ten cents for running errands. It was on one of these errands, when she was eight, that Marian saw a handbill in the grocery store that said, "Come and hear the baby contralto." And there was her picture on the handbill. To her surprise, she was to sing in a church fundraiser.

Upon her father's death, when she was ten, Marian and her family moved in with her paternal grandparents—a rare combination of race and culture. Grandpa was a hardworking, religious man, a convert to the Jewish faith; he called himself a *Black Jew*. Her grandmother was a strict Baptist. She always wanted her grandchildren to remember that she was part *Native American*.

> *"There was no applause at all. What proceeded was a silence, so instinctive, so natural and so intense that it was difficult to breathe..."*

Marian had but one dream in her childhood: to sing on the concert stage. She appreciated her beautiful, unique gift and generously sang at every opportunity. All welcomed her rich voice. Trying to enroll in music school, she was abruptly told, "We don't take colored." This did not dissuade Marian. She continued to study and practice and was soon being paid for her performances.

Members of Philadelphia's Black community began the *Fund for Marian's Future*, which enabled her to study with Agnes Reifsnyder, the most famous contralto in the area. Shortly before graduating from high school, Anderson auditioned for voice teacher, Guiseppe Baghetti, who immediately accepted her as a pupil. Baghetti became Anderson's primary teacher and can be credited with refining her technical skills, expanding her repertoire to include classical songs and arias.

Many opportunities were closed to her because of her race. The New York Herald wrote, after her debut with the Philharmonic Symphony Orchestra at Lewisohn Stadium: "Her voice was rich and powerful, in spite of being a Negro."

It was in Europe that her talent began to be recognized. Marian made her debut in Berlin in 1930. At the Salzburg music festival, she sang *The*

Crucifixion, so brilliantly that an American Journalist, Vincent Sheenan, reported: "There was no applause at all. What proceeded was a silence, so instinctive, so natural and so intense that it was difficult to breathe. She had interpreted the suffering of the cross outside the limits of classical music." Arturo Toscanini attended the concert and told her in the presence of her friends: "Yours is a voice such as one hears once in a hundred years." On hearing her sing, Finnish composer, Jean Sibelius, wrote *Solitude,* especially for her voice.

Back in America, in 1938, The Daughters of the American Revolution forbade her to perform at Constitution Hall, their national headquarters. Eleanor Roosevelt resigned the D.A.R. in protest of this blatant discrimination; other prominent women followed suit. Through Eleanor's influence, on Easter morning, April 9, 1939, Marian sang at the Lincoln Memorial to an enthusiastic crowd of over 70,000. The response to this performance gives us a sense of her enormous singing gift. Four years later, the D.A.R. invited Anderson to take part in a concert for China Relief at Constitution Hall. "There was no sense of triumph," Anderson later wrote, "I felt that it was a beautiful concert hall, and I was happy to sing in it."

On January 7, 1955, Marian became the first black singer to perform as a member of the Metropolitan Opera in New York City, opening the door for other black singers who would follow her. The audience honored her with a standing ovation, *before* she began her performance.

Thousands of words have been written about what Marian Anderson has meant to her country, to her people and to music. It was therefore a natural step on September 10, 1958, for her to be appointed a goodwill ambassador to the United Nations.

The words on the Presidential Medal of Freedom, which she received in 1963, say it best: "Marian Anderson has ennobled her race and her country, while her voice has enthralled the world."

Look for These Traits in Marian's Handwriting

1. Deliberateness: Separated stems, usually in the letters *t* and *d*, slightly rounded at the top, imply that the writer is deliberate and prone to move slowly in carrying out a task.

2. Dignity: When *d*- and *t*-stems are retraced, or partially retraced, dignity is indicated. A high degree of self-worth, repute and honor is implied (see dictionary).

3. Attention, desire for: A desire to attract attention is present if finals rise above the tops of lower case letters or words. When finals turn back, the writer has an excessive desire to be noticed. He or she will constantly find ways to be noticed.

4. Showmanship: Over-sized, flowing and decorative writing especially in capitals shows a flair for dramatization. When done with taste and simplicity, showmanship is indicated.

Marian's handwriting came from a letter written in Helsinki, Finland in 1933.

5. Self-Reliance: Underscored names indicate self-reliance. The writer wants to accomplish her aims without help from others.

6. Rhythm: The regular return of the writing to the baseline, or writing with a beat, suggests that the writer possesses the quality of rhythm. The writer thinks and moves in an orderly manner. Careful spacing of letters also contributes to rhythm.

What Handwriting Reveals About Marian

MUSIC HAS BEEN called *the universal language*. Whether Marian sang in German, Italian or English, the language was not what the audiences heard; it was how she interpreted the music with her voice.

Her handwriting returns consistently to the baseline like a conductor's baton or the *beat* of a drum. She needed this rhythm in her life; she would be comfortable with consistency and repetition. It could be considered a basic requirement in the expression of her talent.

Her great dignity, seen in the retracing of her *t*'s and *d*'s, showed in everything she did: the way she dressed, the way she walked and talked and, most of all, the way she sang. Her gracious appearance was but her soul shining through.

If rhythm is combined with dignity, one could readily see that the predominant themes in her life were the ability to think and act in a smooth, rhythmic manner and her dignity that gave her a sense of intrinsic worth, a quality that culminates in a high degree of self-esteem.

> **Her great dignity, seen in the retracing of her *t*'s and *d*'s, showed in everything she did: the way she dressed, the way she walked and talked and, most of all, the way she sang.**

The underscore of Marian's signature shows that she instinctively relied on herself. This trait is often found in the handwriting of those individuals whose backgrounds provide little financial help. Strong self-reliance gave strength to her desire to achieve.

Marian would not be pushed into a corner; she wanted center stage, in front of an audience. The flourishes, seen in the large capital letters of her signature and the capital *B*'s in her handwriting, indicate this. She was a *showman*. Being the center of attention was the position Marian most desired. However, because of her dignity, she would always observe the rules of decorum and tended to be formal in her manner.

She had the rare quality of never allowing herself to be hurried. We see a perfect example of deliberateness in the separated stem of the *t* in *past*, slightly rounded at the top, which suggests that she was prone to move slowly in carrying out a task. This would add to her dignity and grace.

The rhythm, nobility, and showmanship seen in Marian Anderson's flowing handwriting, give us an insight into her personality, just as her beautiful voice still inspires us.

CHAPTER 2

JOAN OF ARC

1412?–1431

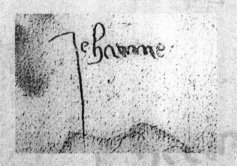

Handwriting can show

if it comes from a person who is

noble minded...

KUO JO-HSU, CHINESE PHILOSOPHER, PAINTER, 1060—1110 AD

THE STORY OF *Joan of Arc, a young medieval woman, has been well-docu-mented. A life, so gallant and so singular, warrants a dedication to the truth. One source made it possible to present a reliable picture of her life as it unfolded: The Jean 'Arc Archives in Rouen, France.*

Joan was born to Jacques and Isabelle d'Arc in Domremy, France. At this point in history, France had been at war with England for nearly one hundred years. The country was divided by chaos and brutality. English soldiers occupied half the nation. Bands of soldiers roamed the countryside, robbing and killing innocent people.

This led Joan's father, a farmer and headsman of the village of Domremy, to organize a group of farmers to obtain a derelict castle in which the villagers took refuge from raids. Joan's family was not wealthy; yet there was no evidence of sordid poverty. As a youngster, she was neither a hero-ine nor a beggar-maid. She worked on the farm, herding sheep. Joan learned domestic skills and religion from her mother. "It was my mother alone who taught me the Our Father, the Hail Mary and the Creed..." (from her testi-mony at her trial). As a child she began to hear what she called *voices*, only she could hear, of St. Michael, St Catherine and St. Margaret; they simply told her to be good, go to church and say her prayers.

Joan had no formal education; she was unfamiliar with the alphabet. She did, however, learn to sign her name as an adult. Many princesses and women of social standing, at that time and in later centuries, were in a sim-ilar position. For instance, when Marie Antoinette was Joan's age, she could not write her name, although she lived in the late 1700s.

Soldiers came to the d'Arc family door, swords in hand, too often to be disregarded. Neither Joan nor her people could afford to be ignorant of what was going on in the feudal world. Joan understood the political and military situation in medieval France.

As she grew older, the voices began to come to her more often. They persisted in telling her to seek out the disheartened Dauphin, the uncrowned king of France, to tell him that he could save France and be crowned King at Rheims Cathedral.

Finally, when an English army laid siege to Orleans, the Archangel told Joan it was time to act. To achieve her goal, Joan, accompanied by her cousin, journeyed to a military fortress at Vaucouleurs and informed its commander, Robert de Baudricourt, of her mission to save France. She requested that he provide her with a squad of soldiers to escort her to the uncrowned king. Baudricourt refused.

Undaunted, Joan remained in Vaucouleurs. While she waited for Baudricourt to change his mind, many in the town were converted to her cause, including some of Baudricourt's officers. They bought her a horse and, at her request, men's clothing. The townspeople began calling her *la Pucelle*—the maid.

Her perseverance was rewarded when she convinced Baudricourt of her divine mission, by telling him of a disastrous defeat of the French army that had taken place the same day at Rouvray-St. Denis, two hundred miles away. Joan's prophecy made a believer of Baudricourt. He authorized the journey and assigned a squad of soldiers to escort her.

Joan had no formal education; she was unfamiliar with the alphabet. She did, however, learn to sign her name as an adult.

On March 9, 1429, Joan was escorted into the Royal Presence. What an awesome scene for a simple farm girl. No fewer than three hundred men surrounded Charles, the Dauphin, in a great hall ablaze with torches. One of the nobles, trying to fool Joan, pretended to be the Dauphin—Joan gave him merely a passing glance. She walked directly to the lean and spindly-shanked Charles, whom she had never seen. History tells us that she said, "Gentle Dauphin, The King of Heaven has announced to me that you will be crowned at the Cathedral in Rheims...I tell you...you are the true heir of France." She convinced him of her mission. Overwhelmed, the Dauphin gave Joan command of his army. He purchased a suit of armor and provided her with a special banner that depicted Jesus with two angels.

The Dauphin had retreated from city to city. The last stronghold was Orleans. Joan proposed and executed a series of bold maneuvers to uphold Orleans for Charles. She took other places along the Loire River, routed the English at Patay and persuaded Charles to march on Rheims where, in the cathedral with Joan by his side, he was crowned King Charles VII of France.

"The man on a white horse" did not come to the rescue of France. It was a chaste, unspoiled young woman of seventeen, dressed in full-plate armor. She inspired the Dauphin's troops with her banner and her noble mission. She was eager to push her victories, which had turned the tide of the Hundred Years War with England (1337–1453).

For a variety of reasons, King Charles undertook negotiations with the Anglo-Burgundians, primarily because the French Royal Court was committed to concluding a peace with the English. Charles later admitted that this was a bad policy.

During these negotiations, Joan was captured by the Anglo-Burgundians, who later transferred her to the English in exchange for the usual monetary compensation. The English not only wanted Joan killed, but also wanted to discredit Charles as a failed king, by having the Church condemn Joan as a witch and a heretic.

In order to accomplish their goals, the English enlisted political and religious figures they knew to be favorable to their cause, the staunchest, of which, was French Bishop Pierre Cauchon who had convinced himself of Joan's guilt. Cauchon was a long-term partisan of the Anglo-Burgundians.

Though betrayed, captured and insulted, Joan held on. She faltered once, but adjusted and carried on, in spite of being told by her visionaries that her end would be soon and hard. She was interrogated in prison, during which time she was harassed and humiliated. Transcripts of her trial show that she always answered in a thoughtful and straightforward manner. When asked about angels, she said: "They come many times among Christians, but are not seen." One judge asked her if she was in a state of grace. "If not, may God put me into it." she said. "Nothing on earth would pain me more than not to be in it. If I were in sin, I believe the voices would not come." The trial, held in 1431 in an ecclesiastical court in Rouen, France, was headed by French Bishop Cauchon and some well-bribed judges. It ended with Joan's condemnation.

On May 30, 1431, to the distress of her soldiers and followers, she was taken to the stake and burned, on charges that were limited to the vague claim that the voices she heard were not those of saints, but rather of demons. A second allegation that she viewed her banner as *magical* was quietly dropped before the end. When the torches set fire to the wood at her feet, she was heard calling out the name *Jesus*.

"The man on a white horse" did not come to the rescue of France. It was a chaste, unspoiled young woman of seventeen, dressed in full-plate armor.

One of the English leaders returned from the execution weeping and groaning, "We are lost. We have burnt a good and holy person." After Joan's death, many of her followers returned to the battle with renewed vigor. By 1453 the last English soldier was driven from France.

After her death, for hundreds of years, in the month of May, blue and white flags flew throughout France in honor of Joan, their national heroine. She was exonerated in 1456 by King Charles and later canonized by the Catholic Church. She is the most notable Warrior-Saint in the Christian calendar.

For most of the French people, the verdict that condemned her to death was irrelevant. They had long since taken Joan into their hearts. They had no trouble accepting her as the bearer of a divine call to justice and peace.

Joan's Signature

The letter dictated and signed by Joan is in Medieval French.

Look For this Trait in Joan's Signature:

Determination:
Heavy downstrokes, descending below the baseline, give evidence of determination; the width or heaviness indicates strength, the length indicates endurance. This is an indication that the writer had firmness of purpose and was resolute.

The English translation is as follows:

Dear and good friends, you well know how the town of Saint-Pierre-le-Moutiere was taken by assault,

and with God's help I intend to clear out the other places which are against the King. But because so

much powder, arrows, and other war material has been expended before the said town and because

myself and the lords who are at this town are so poorly provisioned for laying siege to La Charite,

where we will be going shortly, I pray you, upon whatever love you have for the welfare and honor

of the King and all the others here, that you will aid the siege and immediately send powder, saltpeter,

sulfur, arrows, strong arbalests and other materials of war. And do this so that it will not be prolonged

for lack of the said powder and other war materials, and so that no one can say that you were negligent

or unwilling. Dear and good friends may Our Lord protect you. Written at Moulins the ninth day of November.

Joan.

What Handwriting Reveals About Joan

We had the privilege of viewing two other letters signed by Joan. However, the signature made available to us, the one we are using as our example, is from the letter dictated and signed by Joan to the citizens of Riom on November 9, 1429. This was an incredible find, by scholar Jules Quicherat, in the municipal archives of Riom in the 1830s. The wax of the seal bore a fingerprint and a strand of black hair, believed to be Joan's (the strand of hair has since disappeared). If indeed the fingerprint and strand of hair were Joan's, one can only imagine the impact this would have had on the citizens of Riom to know that this was a letter from La Pucelle, and that it had been signed by her.

The wax of the seal bore a fingerprint and a strand of black hair, believed to be Joan's...

History tells us that Joan learned to write as an adult. Her signature appears to have been executed with difficulty. Critics suggest a forced or assisted signing, but reliable sources tell us otherwise. The letter addressed to the citizens of Riom would have been written with a quill pen on animal skin parchment. Ink used was most likely made from the outer shell of a walnut, mixed with lampblack and Arabic gum.

THE BODY OF the letter, shown here, indicates writing that is markedly different from the signature affixed to it. One hand wrote the letter and another signed it. The Jean d'Arc Archives assured us that it is indeed Joan's signature.

The signature has been reviewed with prudence and discretion, given the circumstances under which the document was signed. The only stroke to be discussed here will be the downstroke of the capital *J* in *Jehanne*. We addressed the unique strokes following the letter *J* and decided to exclude them. As they were written nearly six hundred years ago, to include such strokes would be to indulge in conjecture.

It should be noted that the other two letters that Joan signed and we reviewed were similar in the downstroke of the letter *J* of Jehanne. The stroke is eight times longer than the lower case letters of Joan's writing. The continuation of the stroke, to such a degree, makes it very unique.

Strokes that descend below the base line indicate the trait of determination; no matter how difficult the task or the obstacles faced, the writer will stay the course. This one stroke in Joan's signature is an indication that God had chosen a worthy instrument.

By the length of this determination stroke, one can understand the singularity of purpose in which she restored the Dauphin to his rightful place as King of France...

By the length of this determination stroke, one can understand the singularity of purpose in which she restored the Dauphin to his rightful place as King of France, and the steadfastness with which she led the French army against overwhelming odds. Joan's vision of freeing France from English rule remained long after her physical presence was gone. The king and his soldiers, filled with the memory of her resolve, continued the fight after her tragic death.

A fitting eulogy to Joan of Arc, for the life she lived and the cause for which she freely gave her life, was magnificently expressed in Cervantes' immortal Don Quixote: "To dream the impossible dream, to fight the unbeatable foe, and never stop dreaming or fighting, this is man's privilege and the only life worth living."

It was not a man, but a seventeen-year old girl who carried through to the end, and who demonstrated, in a noble way, the heights to which a human being can rise.

CHAPTER 3
CATHERINE II
1729–1796

There can be no doubt that the handwriting

of a person has some relation

to his mind and character.

WOLFGANG VON GOETHE,

GERMAN AUTHOR, 1749–1832

O N NEW YEAR'S Eve, in 1744, a courier from Empress Elizabeth, of Russia, delivered a letter to the parents of Princess Sophia in the small German principality of Anhalt-Zerbst. The bright and perceptive Sophia, who was just fifteen, was quick to note that her name appeared on the dispatch. She immediately discerned that she was being considered as the future wife of the Grand Duke Peter of Russia. Shortly, thereafter, Sophia unhesitatingly traveled to Russia with her mother, carrying with her three gowns the Empress had provided.

Sophia's intuition was correct. She assumed the name Catherine, upon her engagement to Peter, heir to the throne of Russia. In 1745 the Grand Duke, Peter, and the sixteen-year-old Grand Duchess, Catherine, were married in the most magnificent royal wedding Europe had ever seen.

Historians tell us that Catherine found herself married to a homely, ignorant man, who was impotent, an epileptic and politically inept. Some of his decrees showed foolishness, bordering on insanity. When a rat ran in front of his horse, interrupting military practice, Peter had the rat hung publicly.

Catherine was ignored and neglected by both Peter and the Empress. However, her greatness began to be manifested when she rose to these challenges by pouring herself into strengthening her character and improving her mind.

Catherine was not a beauty and had determined early in life that she must develop her personality. Her unshakable focus was on preparing herself for the future. She became thoroughly Russian and converted to Russian Orthodoxy. Catherine had an insatiable appetite for knowledge. Historians agree that she was never without a book in her pocket. Her intellectual life also orbited around meetings and correspondence with foreign philosophers, such as Voltaire and Newton.

She demonstrated an innate ability to negotiate tactfully, by surrounding herself with capable generals and administrators. Two such people were Suvorov, a dramatic and effective general, and Potempkin, the statesman who advised Catherine on such issues as the annexation of the Crimea.

Catherine was the force behind the building of The Hermitage, the world famous art museum in St. Petersburg. Shortly after her coronation she donated one million rubles for the purchase of major collections of Italian and Flemish art. Catherine loved striding along the lengthy passages between her isolated chambers and the more public halls of the museum, relating how "my little retreat is so situated that to be back and forth from my room takes three thousand steps. There I walk amid quantities of things that I love and delight in, and it is these winter walks that keep me in good health and on my feet."

> *There was nothing petty about Catherine. She herself asserted that it was ambition that sustained her.*

There was nothing petty about Catherine. She herself asserted that it was ambition that sustained her—ambition to excel in everything and bring everything under her control. She wanted big things, and she got them. The expansion of Russia by 600,000 square miles, during her reign, was one example. Purchasing masterpieces for The Hermitage exemplified her need to collect large and impressive items. Each acquisition represented another jewel in the crown of Empress Catherine.

Though it would have been difficult if not impossible to eliminate serfdom in Russia, Catherine had considered the possibility. Shockingly, in 1783, Catherine reversed her position when, with a stroke of the pen, she reduced over three-quarters of a million peasants to serfdom.

Although historical critiques present a negative side of the Empress, with questions about her callous attitude towards the serfs and her lusty personal life, she has her place in history: her achievements set the tone for Russian society well into the Nineteenth Century.

Look for These Traits in Catherine's Handwriting

1. Aggressiveness:
A stroke that swings out boldly from a downstroke points to aggressiveness. The writer pushes forward, strongly resisting anything or anyone who could obstruct a planned course of action.

2. Self-Deceit:
A loop at the left of a circle letter such as *a, d, g,* or *o* indicates self-deception. The writer will not be honest with herself about certain areas of his or her life.

3. Persistence: Tied strokes in *t* and other letters imply persistence. The writer will keep trying after setbacks.

4. Enthusiasm: When a *t*-bar is long, enthusiasm is evident; the longer the bar, the greater the enthusiasm. The writer has a tendency to be eager and intense.

5. Egotism: Very large or tall capitals are evidence of egotism; an inflated opinion of one's self.

Catherine's writing is in archaic French, written in 1763.

6. Acquisitiveness:
Initial hooks in the writing indicate the desire to acquire. Large hooks indicate a desire for important possessions. Small hooks imply that the writer craves trivial things.

7. Tenacity: Final hooks show tenacity. It is the quality of holding fast to what one has: possessions, people, or abstract ideas.

8. Goals: The location of the *t*-bar indicates the goals of the writer (see dictionary). Goals indicate the end the writer wishes to attain.

9. Vanity: Excessively tall *t*-stems indicate vanity, an excessively high opinion of one's ability, appearance, or possessions (see dictionary).

10. Sarcasm: Arrow-like *t*-bars indicate sarcasm. The writer has a tendency to influence the actions of others.

What Handwriting Reveals About Catherine

THE CHARACTERISTICS SEEN in Catherine's handwriting show a woman both forceful and complex. The crossing of the *t* that travels back, loops, and then pushes forward, in a sweeping manner, tells us that Catherine was persistent, strongly self-directed and enthusiastic, traits that enabled her to go forward with great energy, carrying others with her. Her vitality could be instantly recharged, revealed in the heaviness of her handwriting. The aggressive stroke, seen in the *q* of *que*, indicates that Catherine would go after what she wanted with forceful energy.

The aggressive stroke seen in the *q* of *que*, indicates that Catherine would go after what she wanted with forceful energy.

The sharp ending point of the *t*, in Catherine, reveals her propensity to be sarcastic. Although this detracted from her character, it was not without its effectiveness. She could cut down a person with sword-like precision. The weapon of sarcasm was always in its sheath, ready to strike.

Unique hooks are seen throughout her writing, especially in the capital C of Catherine. The beginning hook indicates a desire to acquire, the ending hook, to retain. The need to acquire is magnified by the size of the letter C; it points to her huge ego.

People were impressed by Catherine's poise, bearing and dignity, shown in the retraced *t*'s. The height of the *t*'s shows her pride, which could rise to the point of vanity and was expressed in the way she spoke, dressed and conducted herself.

The Empress' character had one flaw that permeated her entire reign: the tendency to deceive herself about certain unpleasant realities. This was seen in her difficulties with the peasants who became bound to their masters in feudal servitude during her reign and in her romantic dalliances. This self-deception is shown in the initial loop of certain circle letters such as the *a*'s in Manechal.

In summary, Catherine's handwriting reveals an enormous ego that needed constant feeding. She was ambitious, energetic, intelligent, persistent and quick to retaliate; yet she was able to draw people to her, giving Russia a strong and powerful leader. But she had her shortcomings. She was blind to her faults and seemed unwilling to acknowledge her own weaknesses.

CHAPTER 4

MARIE CURIE

1867–1934

Marie Curie with her husband Pierre

It is easier to disguise the meaning

of your words than that

of your handwriting.

The ABC's of Handwriting Analysis, CLAUDE SANTOY,

FRENCH PSYCHOLOGIST, 1994

"My life is such an uneventful, simple little story. I was born in Warsaw of a family of teachers. I married Pierre Curie and had two children. I have done my work in France." This is the self-effacing response of Marie Curie, the winner of two Nobel Prizes, when asked in her later years if she planned to write her autobiography.

Marya Sklodowska was the fifth child of a poor but intellectual family in Poland. Her older sister, Bronya, wanted to become a doctor, whereas Marya dreamed of one day becoming a scientist. Women, in Poland, at that time in history, were prohibited from receiving a higher education. Marya and her sister worked out a plan. Bronya would go to the Sorbonne in Paris, while Marya took a job as a governess, sending money to Bronya for her education. After receiving her degree as a doctor, Bronya, in turn, would help Marya attend the Sorbonne.

Marya was overwhelmed at the sophistication, the new ideas and the freedom of thought and speech she encountered in Paris. It was 1891 when she began her studies at the Sorbonne. She was 24.

Her name soon became Marie, the French version of Marya. Life in France was difficult. Despite living under Spartan conditions and becoming ill on several occasions from lack of food and sleep, in the spring of 1893 Marie graduated first in her class. Her physics professor then gave her an original research assignment. Marie's dream of devoting her life to science was coming true. One year later she received her master's degree in mathematics.

It was during this time that she met Pierre Curie. Pierre, attracted by Marie's beauty, shyness and serious demeanor, saw in her a very unusual woman. His first gift was not roses or chocolates, but a treatise he had prepared: "Symmetry of an Electric Field and of a Magnetic Field." On the flyleaf was written "To Mlle Sklodowska, with the respect and friendship of the author, P. Curie."

Before Marie returned to her beloved Poland, Pierre proposed marriage. She refused. Beautiful, dignified and sensitive letters from Pierre began to arrive in Warsaw. An excerpt from one of these reads: "The prospect of being two months without hearing from you is extremely disagreeable to me. That is to say, a word from you will be welcome...it would be a beautiful thing, which I dare not hope for, if we could pass our lives close to each other, hypnotized by our dreams, your patriotic dreams, our humanitarian dream and our scientific dream." He did not use the word *love,* but his feelings became clear as Marie read between the lines.

Pierre saw the importance of Marie's experiments and abandoned his studies to devote the rest of his life to her research.

Upon her return to France in 1895, Marie, the intelligent and serious scientist, married Pierre, the shy and bright physicist. For their honeymoon they bicycled through France, picnicking as they went. Home for the Curies was a small, three-room apartment in Paris, sparsely furnished with castoffs from friends. Neither wished for anything more. In the middle of the main room was a long table, with Pierre's books and work station at one end and Marie's at the other. There were few, if any, decorations in the rooms. Marie often added a feminine touch with a vase of fresh flowers on the table. This was the setting as they dedicated their lives to research. Their marriage launched one of the most significant partnerships in scientific history.

While Marie was pursuing her doctorate in physics, a French scientist, Henri Becquerel, found that a substance called uranium gave off mysterious rays. Marie determined to make uranium the subject of her doctorate. The birth of their two daughters, Irene and Eve, in 1897 and 1904 did not interrupt Marie's intensive scientific work.

She found that the mineral, pitchblende, contained uranium. Pierre saw the importance of Marie's experiments and abandoned his studies to devote the rest of his life to her research. They confined their study to a painstaking refinement method that required processing tons of pitchblende, trying to answer the question of the mysterious rays.

In just two months of research, she made two important discoveries: the intensity of the rays was in direct proportion to the amount of uranium in her sample, and nothing she did to alter the uranium affected the rays, such as combining it with other elements or subjecting it to light, heat or cold. This led her to formulate the theory that the rays were the result of something happening within the atom itself, a property she called *radioactivity*. One evening, as they sat at home, Marie suddenly felt she must return to the laboratory to check on her experiment. As she and Pierre opened the door of the little shed, they saw a faint but very definite blue glow in the darkness. It was a tiny speck of the radioactive element radium, a substance formed by atomic disintegration.

It took two years to isolate enough radium to confirm its existence. In 1903 Marie and Pierre announced their discovery. Marie earned her doctorate and, together with Pierre and Becquerel, won the Nobel Prize for Physics; the first woman to do so.

Marie and Pierre often became sick, which caused them to tire easily. Large amounts of pitchblende had to be stirred in huge pots for hours at a time. Their fingers cracked with lesions that would not heal. The constant contact with the radioactive element was showing its effects. Seventy-five years after they were written, three of Curie's notebooks were considered too dangerous to handle because of radioactivity.

1906 was a difficult year for Marie. Pierre, her constant companion and support in her scientific endeavors, was killed in an accident in Paris. He absentmindedly stepped into the path of an oncoming horse and carriage. Though grief-stricken, Marie was determined to go on. Soon after the accident, the Sorbonne offered her Pierre's position as head of the Physics Department. She was the first woman in France to receive that honor.

Marie continued with her scientific research. In 1911 she began to share her findings and ideas with Paul Langlevin, a fellow scientist. Their relationship led to a scandal. French newspapers wrote disparaging reports about

Marie. The actual extent of her personal involvement with Paul Langlevin will never be known. The only thing that can be said for certain is that Marie was left with deep emotional scars.

The Nobel Committee notified her that she was to receive her second Nobel Prize, this time in Chemistry. She was the first person, man or woman, to be so honored. However, the Committee suggested she not be present to receive the award because of the Langlevin scandal. Despite a grave illness, the innuendoes of the press and the suggestion of the Committee, Marie attended the ceremonies and accepted the award in person.

The first mobile radiological station came into being. The stretcher-bearers brought in the wounded as Marie stood by the surgeons, many of whom had never heard of X-rays.

For the next few years, Marie's health was precarious but, by the summer of 1913, she felt well enough to take a walking tour in the Swiss Alps. In the party was Albert Einstein. The famed German scientist had a mind so extraordinary that even his learned colleagues had trouble understanding his theories; Marie, however, had no trouble communicating with him.

In 1914 at the beginning of World War I, the city of Paris, in recognition of her contribution to science, founded the Institute of Radium. The Institute buildings remained empty, however, as refugees began to pour into Paris. In the first ten days of warfare, the French Army suffered 300,000 casualties.

By this time, radiology—the study of X-rays—was well advanced. Marie, with the help of the Red Cross, equipped an automobile with radiological equipment. The first *mobile radiological station* came into being. The stretcher-bearers brought in the wounded, as Marie stood by the surgeons, many of whom had never heard of X-rays. The surgeons were soon converted when Marie pointed out the black spots on the X-ray that marked bullet or shell fragments. She trained 150 technicians. It was estimated that

X-rays helped over 1,000,000 wounded Frenchmen, because of Marie Curie and her dedication.

At last, in 1925, Marie's dream came true. She and her sister, Bronya, raised money to construct The Radium Institute in Warsaw. The president of Poland laid the first stone; Marie laid the second.

Soon after, Marie was diagnosed with pernicious anemia. She died in 1934 at the age of 66; the exposure to radioactivity had taken its toll. Marie lived long enough to see her investigation into the *mysterious rays* give birth to an entirely new scientific discipline: atomic physics.

This incredible woman, known as Madame Curie, left her homeland at age 24 and returned as a world famous scientist with many medals and honors. She had become an honorary member of more than eighty scientific societies and the winner of two Nobel Prizes.

In April 1995 Marie's remains, along with Pierre's, were enshrined in the Panthéon in Paris, the memorial to France's great men. Because of her achievements in physics, Marie was the first woman to be so honored.

Look for These Traits in Marie's Handwriting

1. Fluidity: Smooth, flowing strokes connecting words or found in letter structures indicate fluidity. The writer expresses him or herself easily in writing or speaking.

2. Determination: A heavy downstroke below the baseline is an indication of determination. If the stroke becomes heavier at the end, endurance is added. This is an indication of being resolute or having firmness of purpose.

3. Intuition: Frequent breaks between cursive letters are evidence of intuitiveness. It is assumed that the writer has the power to attain direct knowledge without rational thought or inference.

Marie Curie's writing is in Polish; date unknown; The Polish alphabet has 32 letters.

4. Argumentative: If the first upstroke of the letter *p* rises above the tops of the lower case letters, the writer shows argumentativeness. In Marie's case, the *p* is exceedingly high. She would want to discuss or debate an issue.

5. Emotional Depth: Heaviness of the writing implies how deeply an emotional situation will affect the writer. A heavy-line writer experiences life deeply (see dictionary).

6. Emotional Response: The slant of writing determines the emotional response or how quickly a writer responds to outside stimuli. In Marie's case the heart ruled the feelings (see dictionary).

7. Concentration: Small writing suggests habitual concentration. It intensifies everything else in the personality. In Marie's case the lower case letters were small; she had the ability to focus.

8. Resentment: A straight initial upstroke, originating at or below the baseline, indicates resentment or an alertness to imposition.

9. Self-Control: A crossbar bent in a dome-like bow implies a bending of the will. This trait suggests that the writer is trying to overcome a habit or develop a new one.

What Handwriting Reveals About Marie

Although we were unable to get a complete translation of Madam Curie's note, written in Polish, we were able to obtain a synopsis from a Polish woman living in Germany, telling us that it was a letter to the American Red Cross, thanking them for making it possible for Polish immigrants to enter the United States (date unknown).

...bent *t* crossings, indicating a will that has been conquered and controlled.

AT FIRST GLANCE, to the untrained eye, Marie's handwriting appears quite ordinary. It is written in Polish. Upon further investigation we see many strong qualities that indicate an extraordinary woman.

Determination is a heavy downstroke below the baseline. In Marie's case this stroke is long, strong and, at times, nearly doubles its width at its completion. She could dig down inside herself to complete a task. Nothing could stop her. If distractions occurred, she would always come back to her original intent. *No* could be a powerful word in Marie's vocabulary. She was then able to avoid unnecessary interruptions. Add to this the strong, bent *t* crossings, indicating a will that has been conquered and controlled. Her strong determination, when united with a controlled will, produced an irresistible force in Marie's life.

One cannot overlook the fact that Marie used her potential to the fullest. She was agile in thinking, working, speaking and writing, as shown in the fluid stroke connecting two letter structures in the second word of the second line of her Polish script. She performed her duties easily and in high gear. The structure of the *p*, in Marie's handwriting, would ordinarily indicate argumentativeness but, in her case, the exaggerated upstroke of the *p* shows her love of and desire for discussing abstract concepts. It is no wonder that she and Einstein formed such a strong bond—they had much to discuss.

An aptitude revealed in Marie's handwriting that is often associated with a scientific mind is her small writing. This gave her the ability to focus on what she was doing, to the exclusion of all else, a characteristic that would affect everything she did.

Every person has an inner need to realize his or her potential in life, and Marie was no exception. If that need is thwarted, inner resentment can build up in the individual. This trait is seen in several strokes of her writing, but most significantly, in the inflexible initial stroke in the capital *M* in her signature. This could imply a strong sense of injustice rooted in her past. The lower the stroke begins, below the baseline of the writing, the longer this feeling has been harbored. Not being recognized as a Pole in Russian-dominated Poland, and the injustice of not permitting a woman to have an education, must have made Marie's resentment surge. It could well have been the motivating force that carried her to the Sorbonne, where she underwent true hardship and depravation, living on the top floor with none of the conveniences we consider essential today, such as heat and light.

...the injustice of not being permitted to receive an education as a woman, must have made Marie's resentment surge.

Her years of study, research, and dedication were her foundation. Her intuitiveness, seen in breaks between letters in words, would then come into play. She would sense what she had to do next. Add to this her emotional response and intensity, evidenced by the slant and depth of her strokes, and we see the insight and passion needed to carry her scientific dream forward.

Many honors were bestowed on Marie. The fortunes that could have been hers, had she wanted them, did not change her way of life. She remained devoted to the cause of science, preferring the laboratory to a place in the sun. It was Albert Einstein who said it best when he stated, "Marie Curie is, of all celebrated beings, the one whom fame has not corrupted." The smallness of Marie's handwriting made it possible for her to focus on the project at hand; the long, strong downstrokes of her writing gave her the determination and dedication to finish what she started, not thinking of herself, but of a greater cause: Science.

Few contributed more to the general welfare of mankind and to the advancement of science than this modest, self-effacing woman whom the world knew as Madame Curie.

CHAPTER 5

BABE DIDRICKSON ZAHARIAS

1914–1956

Divergence in handwriting is analogous
to divergence in speech...habit firmly controls the hand
as well as the tongue.

ALBERT S. OSBORN, *The Problem of Proof*, 1926

WHEN MILDRED ELLEN Didrickson was in grade school, an admirer said, "Wow, she can hit a ball just like Babe Ruth!" From that day forward, she insisted—with her fists, if necessary—that everyone call her *Babe*, or else.

During a boys' marble tournament at school, Babe's brother, Louis, told Babe that she couldn't enter. She insisted, however, saying that the contest did not say *no girls*. It came down to the last game of the finals, and it was a contest between Mike, in the sixth grade, and Babe, in the second. Mike won the lag. He took careful aim, shot one marble out of the circle, then another; and then he missed. Babe took aim. Out went the first marble, the second, the third, fourth, right down to the seventh. That was it; Babe won the tournament.

Mildred's parents were from Oslo, Norway. Her mother, Hannah, was an accomplished skier and skater. Her father, Ole, worked on an oil tanker. His work took him around the world. When he arrived in Port Arthur, Texas, he decided that this was where he would like to bring his family. Moving a family of three children to a new country was risky, but Hannah, who wanted to help to make her husband's dream come true, scrimped and saved until they had enough to make the trip.

Poppa, as his family fondly referred to him, was a great believer in physical fitness and insisted on healthy bodies. He built a makeshift gymnasium in the back yard of their Beaumont, Texas home for his growing family of seven children. Included was a weight-lifting device, made from an old broomstick and two flatirons. He insisted that both girls and boys need healthy bodies. All seven of the children became outstanding athletes and strong competitors. Oldest brother, Ole, played professional football, Louis was a champion boxer for the Texas National Guard, and only an eye ailment stopped Arthur from a career in professional baseball. All of Babe's sisters were outstanding athletes and, like her brothers, strong competitors. The Didrickson children competed with one another, but always with respect and admiration.

The family was close. They may have lacked money and, indeed, there were few luxuries, but there was no dearth of affection or family spirit. Hannah took in washing, and all the children took turns at the washboard.

Babe loved to boast about her talents and for good reason. She could throw a ball the length of a football field, 100 yards, make 57 of 65 foul shots in basketball and hit a golf ball the length of three football fields. "You name it, I can play it!" she would say. Babe could run, jump, throw the javelin, swim, dive and bowl.

Babe hurtled into national prominence by her phenomenal performance at the 1932 Olympic tryouts in Chicago.

Competitive drive and persistence characterized Babe's life. At thirteen she sewed up potatoes bags, at a penny a bag, eventually making up to sixty cents an hour. She would keep a nickel and put the rest in Momma's sugar bowl. She excelled in anything she put her hands to; her main interest, however, was sports.

At age 14 she became engrossed in the 1928 Women's Olympics. She immediately began rigorous training, preparing herself to compete in the 1932 event. Over the next four years, Babe dreamed of being in the Olympics, spending every spare minute training vigorously to prepare herself for this world event.

Babe hurtled into national prominence by her phenomenal performance at the 1932 Olympic tryouts in Chicago, not as a member of a sponsored team, but as an individual contestant. Spectators in the stands went wild as Babe dashed from one event to another, winning six of the eight events she entered, breaking four women's records and winning the team competition. Babe's one-woman team piled up thirty points. Her nearest competitor was a twenty-two-member team that tallied only twenty-one points. Not surprisingly, she was immediately heralded as *The Wonder Girl*.

Two weeks later Babe emerged victorious at the Olympics in Los Angeles, winning two gold medals in the javelin and the hurdles, and the silver medal for the high jump. Her victories in the javelin and hurdles were world records.

As an amateur athlete in the 1930s, Babe's means of supporting herself in sports were limited; she was forced to turn professional. Babe was put in the position of having to perform in exhibitions and on the vaudeville circuit. Unfortunately, she was not always given the respect due an athlete of her stature. This was difficult for Babe. However, good fortune came her way when she was invited to play golf by sportswriter, Grantland Rice. Though she had played golf infrequently, Babe's natural ability caused Rice to declare that, "she is the longest hitter women's golf has ever seen, for she has a free, lashing style backed up with championship form and terrific power."

Babe was ruled ineligible to play in amateur golf tournaments because of her professional sports activities. In her usual straightforward manner, she entered the men's Los Angeles Open. Remembering her success at the *no girls* marbles tournament as a child, she applied. Unfortunately, this time she was denied success, for she failed to qualify. It was at this tournament, however, that she met George Zaharias, a professional wrestler, whom she later married. Besides being her husband and life companion, Zaharias provided Babe with the financial backing she needed to reclaim her amateur status. She was reinstated an amateur in 1943.

In 1947 Babe became the first American woman to win the Women's British amateur golf title. She then turned professional, winning thirty-four women's professional golf tournaments, including three US Open victories.

In 1950 the Associated Press named her "the greatest female athlete of the first half of the Twentieth Century." One sportswriter called her "the most talented athlete, male or female, the world has ever seen." This may well have been an exaggeration, but no one denied that she was far above average.

In 1953 Babe was stricken with cancer. She faced illness with the same courage and fighting spirit with which she entered every contest in her life.

Surgery only slowed down the disease. George and Babe established the Babe Didrickson Zaharias Fund to support cancer clinics and treatment centers. A trophy was established in her name, to be awarded annually to the woman athlete who had done the most for amateur sports in the United States.

Babe Didrickson died at age 42. She left another enduring legacy: the memory of a tough and gallant spirit. In spite of her weakened condition she returned to win the 1954 US Women's Open by twelve strokes. A museum has been built in Beaumont, Texas, in Babe's honor. It is believed to be the only one built in memory of a female athlete.

In 1950, the Associated Press named her "the greatest female athlete of the first half of the Twentieth Century."

Look for These Traits in Babe's Handwriting

1. Self-Reliance: The underscoring of writing, especially the signature, indicates self-reliance. She would accomplish her aims without help from others.

2. Self-Confidence: Good-sized capital letters indicate confidence in one's self. Strong self-esteem is implied.

3. Diplomacy: When writing tapers toward the end of a letter formation especially in an *m* or *n*, diplomacy is apparent. The writer will use tact in dealing with people.

4. Domineering Nature: Lower case *t*-bars that slant downward and taper to a point, suggest a domineering nature; a tendency to impose one's opinion on others.

5. Will Power: A relatively heavy *t*-bar is evidence of strong will power, such as seen in the *t* of time. This trait implies the strength of purpose of the writer.

Babe's handwriting comes from a letter written to her friend Peg Kirk Bell (date unknown).

6. Rhythm: The regular return of the writing to the baseline, or writing that has a beat, suggests that the writer possesses the quality of rhythm. The writer thinks and moves in an orderly manner.

7. Emotional Response: The slant of the writing determines the emotional response of the writer. In Babe's case, the heart ruled the feelings (see dictionary).

What Handwriting Reveals About Babe

THE BLENDING OF *nature* with *nurture* is exemplified in Babe Didrickson. Nature gave her an incredibly coordinated and near-perfect physical body. This was enhanced by the supportive and competitive nurturing of her family.

Babe had an indomitable spirit. She had great confidence and wanted to do things by herself; she wanted no help. This is seen in the large capitals of letters and the underscore of her signature. The far-forward slant of her script showed her very human and expressive side. Babe would take action while others would stand by.

Her smooth and rhythmic writing that always returned to the baseline showed itself in all of her athletic undertakings; the swing of the golf club, the shooting of a basket or the throwing of a javelin. This rhythm, this measured regularity, was an intricate part of her person, affecting everything she did.

> **The far-forward slant of her script showed her very human and expressive side. Babe would take action while others would stand by.**

She had the ability to direct others to do her will, a strong support for an ambitious woman, like Babe. There is evidence that, in order to defend herself, she would make strong demands of others. She loved force and cared little how it was exhibited, even to the point of domineering to achieve her goal. The sharp downward stroke of the *t* tells us this. Under these circumstances she would use her diplomatic ability to soften the forcefulness of her personality. This is seen in the diminishing *m* in *Xmas* in her writing.

She is best remembered swinging a golf club—winning seventeen tournaments in a row—a winning streak that still remains unmatched by any golfer, male or female. She was a multitalented athlete, with astounding natural ability, one that the world will not soon forget. We see this in her life, and it is verified in her handwriting.

CHAPTER 6

ISADORA DUNCAN

1878–1927

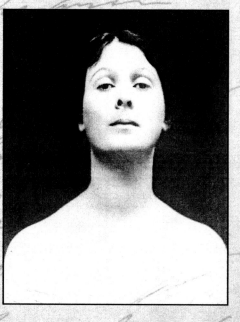

Thomas Gainsborough, English painter, kept the
handwriting of his subject on his easel as he painted.

THOMAS GAINSBOROUGH, 1727–1788

WHEN ASKED WHEN she first began to dance, Isadora would invariably say, "Most probably in my mother's womb."

Born in San Francisco in the late 1800s, the circumstances of Isadora Duncan's life caused her to shoulder financial responsibility for her mother and three siblings at an early age. The constant poverty in which they lived was softened by the wealth of poetry and music that Isadora's mother brought into the home, molding the lives of her offspring. The four Duncan children loved to sing, to play-act and, above all, they loved to dance.

Isadora was a quaint child. She possessed a strange mixture of practical common sense and worldly sophistication, and she hated reality. She was, in fact, a rebel.

Isadora was a quaint child. She possessed a strange mixture of practical common sense and worldly sophistication; she hated reality. She was, in fact, a rebel. Her unhappy childhood was one of strife. Her parents divorced when she was young. Her mother, the seemingly virtuous, highly-principled Victorian lady, who espoused atheism spent many years telling her children what a scoundrel their father was. However, in truth, Isadora found her father to be a charming man and a lovable poet. These contradictions simply heightened her confusion. Passing years tend to soften the intolerance of childhood, but Isadora Duncan never lost her contempt for the institution of marriage, because of what she had witnessed in her childhood. When she was twelve years old she made a solemn vow that she would welcome love when it came, but that she would never marry.

She was a graceful child by nature and, eager to contribute to the family's scarce funds, she began baby-sitting. To amuse the children, she taught them to dance. Matrons in the San Francisco area were pleased, always hoping that their children would gain some of the grace that Isadora exuded.

At age thirteen she fixed her hair in a lady-like bun, at the nape of her neck, and announced to the world that she was sixteen, opening her first school of dance at the old Castle mansion in San Francisco. She taught young hopefuls of society many forms of dance that were fifty years ahead of their time.

Her dances were based on her great love of Greek classical art. Her costume was an adaptation of the Greek tunic. Greek culture and art were popular in America at this time. The fad of *Greek Statue-Posing* allowed *nice* women to shed their corsets, exercise their imaginations and still remain respectable.

Although the timing of her Greek dancing was good, she had little success in the United States. In Europe, however, her triumphs made the name Isadora Duncan famous. She danced in Paris and was cheered; she danced in Berlin where the art-loving Germans went mad with enthusiasm. British royalty honored her, and Vienna took her to its music-loving heart; success and wealth returned for a time. Life was gorgeous. However, it became busy and hectic, full to overflowing and always uncertain. Duncan, the mature dancer, had arrived; yet the little girl, Isadora, was still rebelling against customs, traditions and marriage. Her relationships resulted in the birth of two children.

She opened schools where she taught young girls the beauty of the dance. They would be known as *The Isadorables*. She stated that the purpose of the Isadora schools was "to rediscover the beautiful, rhythmic movement of the human body...Beauty is to be looked for and found in children, whose movements are more beautiful than any string of pearls, belonging to women, who generally sit in the boxes."

Isadora was an innovator and pioneer in expressive dancing. She danced barefoot in her tunic, with colorful scarves draped over her shoulders. When it was suggested that she wear a long dress under her transparent tunic, she rebelled; it would be her way or no way. It was her way.

On one of her return engagements to the United States, where even modest ankles weren't to be exposed, America was shocked, yet delighted.

All gossip ended by an edict from no less a wielder of strong opinion than Teddy Roosevelt: "Isadora Duncan," he proclaimed, "seems to me as innocent as a child dancing through the garden, in the morning sunshine, and picking the beautiful flowers of her fantasy." And, so, Isadora danced, and her sins were forgiven.

Isadora could be found wherever artists, musicians and intellectuals gathered. One of these occasions was at the Bayreuth music festival in Germany. Cosima Wagner, honoring her late husband, composer Richard Wagner, founded the festival. It had become one of Europe's greatest social events, where the wealthy and famous came to see and be seen. King Fredrick I, of Bulgaria, arrived at one of the small gatherings, held during the festival. When the king entered everyone rose, except Isadora, who remained lounged on the couch; she kowtowed to no one.

When the king entered, everyone rose, except Isadora, who remained lounged on the couch; she kowtowed to no one.

It was Wagner's son, Siegfried, an admirer of Isadora, who invited her to the festival. At last Isadora could meet, *in the flesh,* a direct descendent of the composer, whose music she so greatly admired. It was at the festival that Duncan danced to Wagner's *Tannhauser*, a deeply moving opera. She whirled, barefoot, her unbound hair flying, and her white tunic flowing, *intoxicated* by the music. In her words, "My being was vibrating with the waves of Wagner's melody."

When asked to perform in St. Petersburg, Isadora was hesitant, for she wondered how Russians would feel who were accustomed to the gorgeous ballet, with its lavish decorations and scenery. As they watched her dance to Chopin, would her Greek tunic of cobweb and simple backdrop be accepted? This question was answered by a storm of applause that followed her dance.

In the spring of 1916 Isadora performed a charity benefit in Paris for the refugees of World War I. As she danced to the haunting melody of Chopin's *Funeral March*, a vision of tragedy came to her. She danced with her eyes closed and saw her two children threatened by evil. She danced as though in a trance, and her audience sat, thrilled, chilled and breathless; it was terrible, yet beautiful.

When she finished, the audience remained in place for more than an hour, applauding cheering and shouting for encores.

As she had done before, Isadora ended the benefit by dancing to *The Marseilles*, the French National Anthem. The next day a Paris newspaper critic described her performance. "In a robe of red, the color of blood, she stands enfolded. She sees the enemy advance; she feels the enemy as he grasps her throat...and then she rises triumphant with the terrible cry: Aux armes, citoyens! (Arm yourselves, citizens)...She does not make a sound." Spectators were so caught up in the dramatic performance that many thought she was actually carrying a flag, although she used no props. When she finished, the audience remained in place for more than an hour, applauding cheering and shouting for encores.

A few days later, the man who had fathered her son, Patrick, stood before her, his lips dry and his eyes haggard, and told her of the deaths of her two children.

Life was dead; dreams were dead; the world was empty. Isadora, the rebel, had won her rebellion and lost all that might have been worth the fight. She began to travel, trying to distract herself from her grief. Any place would be good, as long as it was *away*. She escaped to Greece and, then, driving restlessly, she went to Italy, Switzerland and France. While in the south of France, she saw a Bugatti car in a shop window and had it sent around for a demonstration.

It was a cool night and Isadora's friends suggested she wear a coat. She rejected such an undramatic idea, flung her red-fringed shawl around her neck, jumped into the low-slung vehicle and struck a mock-heroic pose. With great theatrics she said, "Adieu, mes amis, je vais a la gloire!" (Farewell friends, I go to glory).

The powerful little car sprang forward and then jerked to a halt. To everyone's horror, the fringe of her long, red shawl was tightly entangled in the spokes of one of the rear wheels. Isadora's neck was broken; her head slumped on her chest.

She touched many people in her short life: kings, artists, composers, the wealthy and the prominent, some with scorn and some with delight, yet all with fascination. Her flair and freedom of expression depicted a woman who lived and danced with abandon. Isadora's interpretive and impressionist methods paved the way for dancers and choreographers for years to come.

Look for These Traits in Isadora's Handwriting

1. Emotional Response: The slant of the writing determines emotional slant. A far-forward slant demonstrates that the heart rules the feelings (see dictionary).

2. Stubbornness: A tent-like formation often seen in a *t*. The writer will resist an effort to change.

3. Determination: Long downstrokes below the baseline often seen in the letters *y* and *g*. The writer shows an indication of being resolute or having firmness of purpose.

4. Resentment: A straight initial upstroke, originating at or below the baseline, indicates resentment. The writer will be alert to imposition.

5. Defiance: If the upper part of the *k*, such as in the word *kiss*, rises above the lower case letters in the writing, defiance is indicated. The writer is resistant to authority or opposition.

Isadora's writing is a letter written to Victor Seroff (date unknown).

6. Argumentative: When the upstroke of the letter *p* is higher than the lower case letters in the writing, the writer tends to be argumentative. The writer will want to discuss or debate an issue.

7. Self-Reliance: When the signature is underscored, self-reliance is shown. The writer wants to accomplish his or her aims without help from others.

8. Dignity: When *d*- or *t*-stems are retraced, dignity is indicated. The writer can show a high degree of self-worth, repute or honor (see dictionary).

What Handwriting Reveals About Isadora

Isadora's writing is comprised of excerpts from a letter written by Isadora to Victor Seroff in September 1927 while she was in Nice, France. The entire letter is reproduced in his book, The Real Isadora.

Sunday, September 11/27

Darling Vitia

        Why no letter?

No telegram?

Nothing from you—

I was very anxious

There are a...

inspired moments

in life and the

rest is Chipuka [*Nonsense in Russian*]

I kiss you tenderly

with all my love

Isadora

ISADORA REACTED IMMEDIATELY when her emotions were stirred, seen in the far-forward slant of her handwriting. This reaction was so intense that it overwhelmed her audience. They were with her completely, as she interpreted the music in her dance, combining dignity, shown in the retraced *t*'s, with grace and elegance, seen in the flow of her writing.

Although her emotional response was immediate, it was not long-lasting, revealed in her light writing. She was like a butterfly, flitting from one emotional situation to another. She had her highs and lows. When down, she could be completely down.

Isadora would finish what she had started, seen in the long, enduring strokes descending below the baseline of her script. She would continue on

She was like a butterfly, flitting from one emotional situation to another.

when others would have stopped. The underscore of Isadora's signature tells us that she relied completely on herself.

The defenses she used to resist the restraints that constantly challenged her desire to be autonomous are ever present. Right or wrong, this is how she lived. The forces that drove Isadora, and which are clearly evident in her handwriting, are as follows:

She was resentful: Always on guard against imposition (inflexible initial strokes).

She was defiant: A resistance to authority or opposition (large lower case letter *k* as in the *k* of *kiss*).

She was stubborn: Unbending and inflexible (tent like *t* structures).

She was argumentative: Need to defend ideas and actions (*p*'s which rise above the lower case letters as in *Chipuka*).

As we look at her script we see that Isadora was ready to take on the world—and she did—starting in San Francisco and continuing through Europe with exciting, innovative, yet traumatic experiences. She was always on stage, challenging the mores of the day, whether it be through her dancing or her personal life.

> She was always on stage, challenging the mores of the day, whether it be through her dancing or her personal life.

It could be said that Isadora, the mother of modern dance, loved life with tremendous feeling, always searching for more, never completely satisfied. Her life and her handwriting verify this. She was a temperamental artist of many moods, sometimes extreme, always unpredictable. She defied traditional dancing and always expected her actions to be forgiven. The one, pure and unadulterated emotion Isadora found and kept, the one that she left to the world was in her dancing.

CHAPTER 7

AMELIA EARHART

1897–1937

The best witness is the written paper.

CARL SANDBURG, AMERICAN POET, 1878–1967

Left 7:15..................
Over fog 7:40.................
Rain 7:57....................
8,500 feet...................
Icebergs.................
Fishing boat 9:05.................
Altimeter out............

IMAGINE THE SCENE: the cockpit is cramped; so many things demand constant attention—changing weather, complex controls, blurred sights and unnerving sounds—yet the urge to record what she sees is compelling. Amelia Earhart's writing, scribbled in pencil, suggests she likely wrote holding her notebook on her lap, while all around her challenges loomed. The scrawled entries covered only a few pages in her five-by-two-inch logbook. The year was 1932. She would be the first woman pilot to fly solo across the Atlantic.

The log tells a grueling tale. The plane's altimeter stopped working; in the dark she could only guess her altitude. She flew through fog, and then a storm caused ice to form on her tachometer, sending its needle spinning. With her equipment failing and the storm reducing visibility to zero, she was no longer certain if she was on course or how far she had flown.

The plane's exhaust manifold cracked. Flames pierced the night skies. Ice formed on the Vega's wings, sending it into a spin. Amelia pulled out of the spin, so close to the water that the waves breaking looked close enough to touch.

Again and again she climbed high enough to use her instruments and then descended as the ice thickened on her windshield. Undaunted, she went forward, not knowing her direction. She had been in the air fifteen hours. The fuel gauge was leaking; she knew she must put down soon. She spotted a ship, then a fishing fleet and, at long last, land. The first green pasture that presented itself became a landing field for Amelia's limping Vega. Her destination had been Paris. She landed on the northern tip of Ireland.

"Where am I?" she asked an astonished Dan McCallion who was herding cows.

"In Gallagher's pasture," he said, and then asked her, "Have you come far?"

"From America."

"Holy Mother of God," said McCallion, shocked that a woman had landed a plane in his neighbor's field, and even more shocked that she was wearing pants.

> *Making this incredible trip by herself was not an issue with Amelia. She was comfortable being alone.*

Making this incredible trip by herself was not an issue with Amelia. She was comfortable being alone. The isolation of the small cabin did not create a problem. Amelia prided herself on traveling light; a can of tomato juice and a thermos of soup would sustain her. Since she did not drink tea or coffee, smelling salts kept her awake.

She had broken several records on the flight: the first woman to fly solo across the Atlantic, the only person to fly it twice, the longest non-stop distance flown by a woman and the shortest crossing time.

After the Atlantic solo, European dignitaries wined and dined Amelia, hosting parties and dinners in her honor. She then returned to a ticker tape parade in New York. President Hoover presented her with a Special Gold Medal from the National Geographic Society. She was voted The Outstanding Woman of the Year. The French press ended an article about Amelia's accomplishment with, "but can she bake a cake?" Her response to this was that she accepted her awards on behalf of all women—cake bakers as well as all women who fly.

Amelia Mary Earhart was born in 1897 in her grandparents' home in Atchison, Kansas, where her grandfather, Alfred Otis, was one of the leading citizens. Edwin Earhart, Amelia's father, remained with his law practice in Kansas City during this period. A sister, Muriel, was born two years later. Amelia and Muriel knew privilege and wealth in the years they spent with their grandparents. They attended private schools and basked in many comforts of life.

When Edwin's law practice failed, he took an executive job in Des Moines, Iowa. The girls and their mother joined him there in 1908. Unfortunately, their family situation eroded. Edwin was never able to earn enough to provide the standard of living the girls had enjoyed with their grandparents. Amelia's mother, Amy, used some income from a trust fund to send the girls to private, intermediate schools in preparation for college.

Amelia's favorite subjects were Latin and Mathematics. She preferred geometry; algebra was too easy because she could do it in her head. While going through some of Amelia's belongings from her school days, her sister, Muriel, found an old notebook with yellowed news clippings about women's achievements in fields usually considered a man's domain: a woman doctor, a woman lawyer in Bombay, a woman bricklayer from Toronto, a woman bank president, and others. These preserved clippings suggest her independent spirit, and where the future would lead her.

During her first year at preparatory school, the United States entered World War I. She felt her services were needed in the war effort so, while visiting her sister in Canada, she joined the Voluntary Aid Detachment, which sent her to a Military Hospital. She met a number of pilots during her stay at the hospital. Many had been shot down during reconnaissance flights over enemy territory. Others crashed in training maneuvers. They all had had many brushes with death. This contact piqued her curiosity about aviation.

In the fall of 1919 Earhart enrolled as a pre-med student at Columbia. Although doing well in her studies, in 1920 she decided to join her parents in California.

Her interest in aviation began to bloom. She attended an air show in Long Beach, California, and was fascinated by the exhibition of stunt flyers who raced and performed wing-walking and other mid-air acrobatic tricks.

Three days after the show, her father bought her a ticket for a plane ride. She later recalled, "As soon as we left the ground, I knew I...had to fly."

Neta Snook, the woman who was to be her first flight teacher, recalls the following incident: "A tall, slender young lady and an elderly man approached. She was wearing a brown suit, plain but of good cut. Her hair was braided and neatly coiled around her head. There was a light scarf around her neck, and she carried gloves. She would have stood out in any crowd. The gentleman with her was slightly gray at the temples and wore a blue serge business suit. He walked erect with a firm step. 'I'm Amelia Earhart and this is my father...I want to learn to fly, and I understand you teach students...Will you teach me?'"

> *"I'm Amelia Earhart and this is my father...I want to learn to fly, and I understand you teach students...Will you teach me?"*

In January 1921 Amelia began taking lessons from Snook. Aviation was a man's profession, and Amelia's femininity surprised even her instructor. After a failed takeoff, Snook turned to see the young pilot, with compact in hand, powdering her nose.

Amelia worked at several jobs to pay for her training, which cost $1.00 a minute. She took a streetcar and then walked three miles to reach the airfield for her lessons. On May 15, 1923, she received her pilot's license, one of only sixteen female pilots in the world. She was just shy of her twenty-sixth birthday.

Earhart set a woman's altitude record—14,000 feet without bottled oxygen—while still a student pilot. This feat was accomplished shortly after she had raised the money to buy her own plane, a small Kinner biplane, which she named *The Canary*.

On October 27, 1926 her life was to change forever. A phone call from Captain H.H. Railey asked, "How would you like to be the first woman to fly across the Atlantic?"

George Palmer Putnam, a New York publisher, had asked Railey to find a woman to make a transatlantic flight. She would accompany two male aviators. Railey was struck by Amelia's strong resemblance to Charles Lindbergh and coined the name *Lady Lindy*.

In 1928 Commander Richard Byrd, the Arctic explorer, was made technical consultant for the flight. Wilmer Stultz and Louis Gordon would pilot the tri-motor Fokker named *Friendship*, while Amelia, who had no experience with multi-engines or instrument flying, was given the official title of *Commander* of the flight. She would receive world recognition for this accomplishment.

Amelia was distressed that, after the flight, Stultz and Gordon received no recognition and were ignored by reporters. It was the woman they came to see or rather, *the girl*, as they insisted on calling her. Even President Coolidge cabled his personal congratulations to Amelia.

She went on to London, then the States, conducting a full calendar of tours. Amelia was in great demand on the lecture circuit, and newspapers loved to feature her pictures. Behind the scenes, Putnam kept Amelia's name and accomplishments in the forefront of everyone's mind and in the pages of newspapers across the country.

George Palmer Putnam was a dynamic, handsome man. Their relationship developed until Amelia, having received six proposals of marriage, finally accepted.

George and Amelia were married in 1931. That spring they began making plans to duplicate Charles Lindbergh's 1927 Atlantic solo flight, with Amelia at the controls. With the genius of Putnam's promotion, she made the transatlantic flight in 1932, just five years after Lindbergh. This put her on the front pages of the world's newspapers. Simply put, she had become a famous woman.

Aviation was quite a new concept, and the industry was looking for ways to improve its image. Amelia was appointed Assistant to the General Traffic Manager at Transcontinental Air Transport (later TWA), with the special responsibility of attracting women passengers.

She organized a cross-country air race for women pilots known as the Los Angeles to Cleveland Women's Air Derby. Will Rogers called it *The Powder-Puff Derby,* and the name stuck.

Amelia Earhart's popularity, her bobbed hair, her trousers, her tailored clothes, and her debonair style made launching a fashion house, in 1934, a natural step. The clothes, which sold at Macy's, were her original design. They were sensible, classic-line clothes: shirt-waisted dresses, silk shirts, and slacks with permanent pleats. The whole effect was quiet and tasteful. There were a few original aviation themes, such as tiny silver propellers as buttons, and parachute silk used for blouses. Her label displayed her unique signature, with a line and plane ascending into the sky. She abandoned the fashion house venture, however, to return to her first love—the air. But her time in the fashion spotlight was not without benefits; the exposure she gained in this fashion venture added greatly to her public appeal.

We see many contrasts in this woman. On the one hand, we have the tomboyish, daredevil aviatrix and, on the other, the designer of glamorous women's fashions. Her approach was considered masculine for the era. As an aviatrix, she had the foresight and courage to invade a field that was considered appropriate for men only.

Plans were in motion for her to circle the globe at the equator, a feat never accomplished by man or woman. On the morning of July 2, 1937, Amelia Earhart started the engines of the sleek, silver Lockheed Electra, with her navigator, Fred Noonan, at her side. They left the island of Lae, in New Guinea, bound for Howland Island, a 2,556-mile journey. This was the longest and last leg of their circumnavigation of the world. She had confided to a reporter that it would be her last stunt. Afterward, she would enjoy a quiet life.

That dream never happened. Those who watched her leave Lae, that misty morning, were the last ever to see Earhart or Noonan. Somewhere over the Pacific, the plane disappeared.

The mystery surrounding her disappearance is awash with question marks. Was she using this flight as a spy mission for the US Government?

After all, the Japanese bombed Pearl Harbor just three and a half years later. What about rumors of radio messages heard months after her disappearance? There have been no concrete answers to these questions. One can only speculate as to her fate. The one thing that can be said, with certainty, is that flying made Amelia famous; disappearing made her legendary.

> *The one thing that can be said with certainty is that flying made Amelia famous; disappearing made her legendary.*

Look for These Traits in Amelia's Handwriting

1. Temper: A relatively heavy *t*-bar at the right of the *t*-stem indicates temper.

2. Deliberateness: Separated stems, slightly-rounded at the top, imply that the writer is deliberate or prone to move slowly in carrying out a task.

3. Initiative: An upstroke, above the base-line, that leaps sharply forward from the preceding downstroke indicates initiative.

4. Goals: The location of the *t*-bar in relation to the *t*-stem is one of the ways that a writer reveals his or her goals (see dictionary). Goals indicate the end the writer wishes to attain.

5. Space: The greater the space between letters, words and lines, the more the writer needs his or her private space.

6. Caution: Words ending with a straight stroke, usually at the end of a line, indicate caution. The writer considers carefully before taking action.

7. Intuition: Frequent breaks between cursive letter structures give evidence of intuition. It is assumed that the writer has the power to attain direct knowledge without rational thought or inference.

Amelia's handwriting comes from her log book written on her flight over the Atlantic in 1932.

What Handwriting Reveals About Amelia

AMELIA'S PASSION FOR flying and the solitude she experienced in the air are seen in her handwriting in a unique way. There is an aesthetic balance of space; space between letters, space between words and space between lines. She wanted *elbow-room*. What better place to distance herself from others than in the air. This quality in her handwriting gave her clarity of thinking; the solitude gave her time to think clearly. However, the love of *elbow-room* tended to make her unapproachable, distant.

Amelia's *t*-bars, although varied, were always crossed with pressure, showing her strength of will.

The light of the fire of adventure showed itself in her writing by the *t*-bars that are written above the *t*-stem. She reached out for the unattainable. Amelia's *t*-bars, although varied, were always crossed with pressure, showing her strength of will.

Her handwriting is done quickly, with many breakaway strokes, shown in the *h*'s of her writing. Amelia would not wait for opportunity to find her; if it knocked, she would be there. Amelia had the added strength of intuitiveness that can exert a strong influence on an individual who shows initiative. With the keen insight that comes with intuition, she could sense the moment and seize it.

There is an unusual stroke in Amelia's writing. It occurs in such words as *off*, where the upper stems are made without retracing. This is a sign of being deliberate. She would weigh issues before coming to a final decision. Because of this she could face finality without trepidation. She would understand a matter, having pondered it beforehand.

The approach strokes of many of Amelia's letters tend to *take-off* above the baseline of the writing, as shown in the *f* of *flight* and the *l* of *load*. However, these strokes always return to the baseline. She had her head in the clouds but her feet were firmly on the ground.

Traits seen in handwriting do not always show in the writer's behavior. However, given the right set of circumstances, a trait can surface. Such could be the case in the temper stroke in Amelia's handwriting, seen in the strong *t*-bar, which appears after the *t*-stem. This suggests that Amelia could be angry with herself, should she fail to reach her goals. In circumstances of this nature, temper could become an ally, helping her to fight for things important to her. Because this inner drive could get out of hand, she developed the much needed sense of caution, seen in the lines that stretch-out from final strokes.

The challenge of Rudyard Kipling's words, "If you can fill the unforgiving minute with sixty seconds worth of distance run...," was met by Amelia Earhart.

The challenge of Rudyard Kipling's words, "If you can fill the unforgiving minute with sixty seconds worth of distance run...," was met by Amelia Earhart. This is the way she lived. In her words: "I flew the Atlantic because I wanted to...to want in one's heart to do a thing for its own sake; to enjoy doing it; to concentrate all one's energies upon it...that is not only the surest guarantee of success— it is being true to oneself." The spirit of adventure that sent Amelia Earhart into the air is clearly seen in her handwriting.

CHAPTER 8

HELEN KELLER

1880–1968

Helen Keller and Alexander Graham Bell

Helen Keller

Beauty is God's handwriting.

FRANK WALDO EMERSON, AMERICAN POET, 1803–1882

HELEN KELLER WAS asked in her seventies, "Do you believe in life after death?" "Most certainly," Helen declared, "It is no more than passing from one room to another." Then she added. "But in that other—room—I will be able to see."

Helen's life was unique. When she was 18 months old, an illness left her with only three of her senses: taste, touch and smell. She was blind, deaf and mute. Unlike the rest of us, she was not affected by what she saw or heard and, as a consequence, this gave her a rare insight, allowing her interior life to grow immeasurably.

In her words: "Our blindness changes not a whit the course of inner realities. Of us (the blind) it is as true as it is of the seeing, that the most beautiful world is entered through the imagination. If you wish to be something you are not—something fine, noble, good—you shut your eyes—and for one dreamy moment you are what you long to be."

Helen's mother, Kate, read in Charles Dickens's book, *American Notes*, about the fantastic work that had been done with a blind and deaf child, Laura Bridgman. Although the Kellers had taken Helen to be examined by many specialists, the opinion was always the same. Nothing could be done to restore Helen's sight. Kate then sought advice from a specialist, in Baltimore, who advised her to visit a local expert on the problems of deaf children. This expert was Alexander Graham Bell. Bell was concentrating on what he considered his true vocation: the teaching of deaf children. He suggested that she write to The Perkins Institute for the Blind, in Massachusetts, requesting a teacher for Helen.

Anne Sullivan was the recommendation by Perkins. Anne had been nearly blind, herself; two operations on her eyes led to her regaining enough sight to read normal print, for short periods of time. A recent graduate of Perkins Institute, Anne was finding it difficult to find employment. When she heard of the opportunity to teach Helen, she accepted without hesitation. And so, although she was an inexperienced teacher, fate had intervened; Anne and Helen found each other.

After initial difficulties with this wayward six-year old, Anne capitalized on the sense of touch and, with the use of her fingers, *spoke* to Helen by using the manual alphabet. At this point, however, Helen could only mimic the *finger* words, but not understand their meaning.

It was at Helen's family home in rural Alabama that Anne made the first breakthrough, while leading Helen to the water pump. Helen recounted the *miracle* of those moments later, in these words: "We walked down the path to the well house, attracted by the fragrance of the honeysuckle with which it was covered. Someone was drawing water, and my teacher placed my hand under the spout. As the cool water gushed over one hand, Anne spelled into the other the word *water,* first slowly, then rapidly. I stood still, my whole attention fixed upon the motions of her fingers. Suddenly I felt a misty consciousness, of something forgotten, a thrill of returning thought and, somehow, the mystery of language was revealed to me."

Immediately, she asked Anne (by pointing) for the name of the pump to be spelled out in her hands and, then, the name of the trellis. All the way back to the house Helen learned the names of everything she touched and also asked for Anne's name. Anne spelled the name *teacher* on Helen's hand. Within the next few hours Helen learned the spelling of thirty new words. Once her mind was opened, Helen's desire to learn was insatiable. She could be seen walking through the house, her fingers flying together as she repeated what she had learned that day. To compensate for her disability, she devised sixty distinct gestures to indicate family members and favorite foods.

The rural setting of the Keller home gave Anne the opportunity to teach Helen the smell and feel of flowers, trees, and animals, always taking her mind where it wanted to go. Anne would become exhausted, however, continually having to broaden her knowledge to satisfy Helen's great appetite for learning. With rare insight Anne was slowly bringing the world into Helen's mind. The child's memory was retentive and her curiosity boundless. She quickly caught on to the relationship between things; it was as though she possessed a sixth sense. Helen seemed to *know* what was happening. In Anne's words: "She had never been told anything about death or the burial of a body and, yet, on entering a cemetery to observe some flowers, she laid her hand on her eyes and repeatedly spelled, "cry—cry." Her eyes filled with tears. The flowers did not seem to give her pleasure, and she was very quiet while we stayed there."

Anne taught Helen square-hand pencil writing, as taught at the Perkins Institute. This is a system of printed letters made with the aid of a grooved guide and a pencil. With patience and practice it was possible for a blind person to form letters in block fashion, much like the squared letters and numbers of a digital clock. A pen could not be used because the ink supply could run out, whereas, a pencil could be felt and sharpened at will. Helen also learned to write in Braille and became very proficient on the Braille typewriter, as well as on the classic typewriter. She seldom made a mistake while typing. A typing mistake could be disastrous for a blind person. How could he or she *see* that a mistake had been made?

She seldom made a mistake while typing. A typing mistake could be disastrous for a blind person. How could he or she see that a mistake had been made?

Helen accomplished many of the goals she set for herself. However, despite enormous effort, her most cherished dream of speaking clearly was never realized. When first meeting someone, she would lightly touch the outline of his or her face. Helen's touch felt like the softness of a cobweb brushing by. Having perceived in her mind the image of the individual, she would then place her thumb and fingers on the person's vocal chords and lips, while Anne spelled into her other hand. This technique would help her understand the words being spoken.

Helen and her teacher spent four winters at Perkins as guests, where she expanded her knowledge. She learned to model in clay. She took lessons in French and was tutored in Greek. Helen particularly loved foreign languages.

The authorities at Perkins were keen to promote Helen because of her astonishing progress. Her ability to learn had far exceeded anything anybody had seen before in someone without sight or hearing. She was a phenomenon. Articles were written about her, leading to a wave of publicity. Helen had become famous.

> *Helen faced the terrors of the unknown and mastered them. She learned to swim, to ride a bicycle and to ride a horse.*

She moved on to the Cambridge School for Young Ladies in 1896 and, in the autumn of 1900, entered Radcliff College. She became the first blind and deaf person to enroll at an institution of higher learning. Helen graduated on June 28, 1904, with a Bachelor of Arts degree. Life at Radcliff was very difficult for Helen and Anne. The huge workload led to deterioration of Anne's eyesight.

In her world travels Helen met many illustrious and famous people: Mark Twain, Carl Sandburg, Andrew Carnegie, Thomas Edison and King George VI and Queen Mary of England, to name a few. They wanted to meet this woman who had overcome such adversities and were charmed by her naturalness.

With a rare combination of courage, intelligence and sensitivity, Helen faced the terrors of the unknown and mastered them. She learned to swim, to ride a bicycle and to ride a horse. She flew in an open cockpit airplane and went on camping trips. She was never known to shirk from danger.

In 1922 Anne fell ill and was unable to continue the strenuous activities in which Helen was always involved. By the summer of 1925 Anne's eyesight had deteriorated to the point where Polly Thomson, who had worked for Helen and Anne as a secretary, took on Anne's role. In 1936, Anne died. Helen had known that she would lose her lifelong companion, but the knowledge of it made it no easier. She was emotionally shattered. "The light, the music, and the glory of life had been withdrawn," she wrote later.

Many thought that the death of Anne Sullivan would be the end of Helen's public life. They were mistaken for, with Thomson at her side, she continued to write and travel. In 1937 she and Polly left for the Orient, beginning what would be the first of many world tours. Upon their return, they moved to Arcan Ridge in Westport, Connecticut. This would be Helen's home for the rest of her life.

In 1957 *The Miracle Worker* was first performed, a drama portraying Anne Sullivan's success in communicating with Helen as a child. In 1959 it was re-written as a Broadway play and opened to rave reviews. In 1962 it was made into a film, and the actresses playing Anne and Helen both received Oscars for their performances.

Her last years were not without excitement for, in 1964, President Lyndon Johnson awarded Helen the Presidential Medal of Freedom, the United States' highest civilian award. A year later she was elected to the Women's Hall of Fame at the New York World's Fair.

On June 1, 1968, at Arcan Ridge, Helen Keller died peacefully in her sleep. She was 88. Helen's final resting place, next to her teacher Anne Sullivan, is a popular tourist attraction. The bronze plaque, erected to commemorate her life, has the following words written in Braille: *Helen Keller and her beloved companion, Anne Sullivan Macy.* So many people have visited the chapel and touched the Braille dots that the plaque has already been replaced twice.

Helen, through the books she wrote and her public appearances, profoundly altered the world's treatment and education of the handicapped. Her demonstration of the power of the human spirit over the most crushing adversities, has inspired the world for over a century.

Footnote: If Helen Keller were alive today, her life would have been completely different. Teaching methods now exist that would have allowed Helen to realize her dream of being able to speak. Technology now enables blind and blind-deaf people, like Helen, to communicate directly and independently with anyone, anywhere. However, in reviewing her life we see how, even without modern technology, but through her example, she has shown millions of people that disability need not be the end of the world.

Look for These Traits in Helen's Handwriting

1. Cultural Desires: If the *e* is written in the form of a Greek *e*, cultural and literary aptitudes are evident. This Greek e letter structure may be found in other letters such as *r*. The writer desires refinement of thought, emotions, manners and taste.

2. Pride: Tall *d*- and *t*-stems usually give evidence of pride, but in Helen's case, it is in the tallness of other letters such as *h*, and *l*, where pride is indicated. The writer has a sense of her own dignity or self-worth (see dictionary).

3. Thinking, quick: Retraced, needle-like strokes that are usually seen in *m*'s and *n*'s, in Helen's case, are found in the letters *r* and *p* (penetrating upward, and outside the square). The longer the needle, the more the writer fully comprehends the subjects.

4. Determination: Heavy downstrokes, below the baseline, give evidence of determination. Note the downstroke of *r* in *Keller*, of her signature. The width or heaviness of the stroke indicates strength; the length, endurance. The writer can be resolute or have firmness of purpose.

5. Defiance: The buckle of the *k* should be in the lower case area. When it rises above this area, defiance is indicated. The writer can show a resistance to authority or opposition.

6. Thinking, independent: If the *t*- and *d*-stems are short, in proportion to the rest of the writing, there is evidence of independent thinking. The writer arrives at conclusions without being influenced by other people's opinion (see dictionary).

The Perkins Institute gave us permission to use excerpts of this letter written by Helen when she was eleven years old. The maturity of her personality was already showing itself.

What Handwriting Reveals About Helen

Square-hand writing as taught at the Perkins School was accomplished with the use of a grooved guide, much like a corrugated washboard, and a soft pencil. The student would place a sheet of paper over the guide and would then use the forefinger to press the paper into the groove making a roadway in which to write. Letters within a word would be covered by the left forefinger as soon as made. The forefinger was also used as the space between letters.

Helen, with determination, would finish the task, which shows itself in the long follow-through in the *r*'s of her handwriting.

IN 1951 ELSIE Hurlburt Simonds, referring to square-hand pencil writing, said to the Harvard Class of the Perkins Institute for the Blind: "It is surprising how much individuality the pupils put into the writing of letters made from these set rules. No two children write alike...some write with a graceful backward slant. If a pupil shows a tendency to make slanting lines, he is encouraged to do so."

We often think of defiance as a negative or rebellious trait, but in Helen's case it was her driving force—she defied her disability. She stood up for her rights. She protected her autonomy by fighting her disability. Lesser people would have given up. The strokes of the letter *k* show us her ability to fling down the gauntlet. Regardless of how rough the going became, Helen, with determination, would finish the task, which shows itself in the long follow-through in the *r*'s of her handwriting.

Thinking patterns are difficult to analyze in square-hand pencil writing because, by necessity, the writing strokes are squared. Yet, the penetrating points above such letters as the *r* and *p* (outside the square) show a strong desire to search for knowledge. This stroke made it possible for her to form fast mental decisions.

Helen's handwriting shows a strong desire for cultural and artistic leanings in the formation of Greek *e*'s and in the letter *r*, which also becomes a Greek *e*. This cultural desire developed into a love of fine literature, music and art.

The tall letters of Helen's writing indicate pride, which would inspire respect and admiration from her associates. She was also independent, seen in the short *t* and *d* stems. Helen would not permit herself to be restricted or limited by the dictates of social custom. And so, rather than following conventional patterns, she, out of necessity, would achieve her goals in an independent manner. A deaf-mute, dancing or riding a horse, was unheard of until Helen attempted it.

Her handwriting and her life give us a penetrating view of who she was. Helen Keller expressed it best when she said: "Life is a daring adventure, or it is nothing."

CHAPTER 9

ANNE MORROW LINDBERGH

1906–2001

Anne Morrow Lindbergh

Beware of the man whose writing sways
as the reed in the wind.

CONFUCIUS, CHINESE ETHICAL TEACHER, 551– 479? B.C.

ANNE, WHOSE FATHER was the American ambassador to Mexico, met Charles Lindbergh, the famous aviator, while visiting her family on a break from Smith College in 1927. She wrote in her diary, "I want to marry a hero." And, to her great surprise, she did.

One cannot think of Anne Morrow Lindbergh without immediately remembering that tragic night in 1932, when her twenty-month-old child, Charles A. Lindbergh Jr., was kidnapped, ransomed and brutally murdered.

Anne's words on the pain of loss show her character: "Courage is a first step, but simply to bare the blow bravely is not enough. Stoicism is courageous, but it is only a halfway house on the long road. It is a shield, permissible for a short time only. In the end one has to discard the shield and remain open and vulnerable. Otherwise, scar tissue will seal off the wound, and no growth will follow. To grow, to be reborn, one must remain vulnerable and open to love, but also hideously open to the possibility of more suffering."

The tragic loss of her child devastated this delicate, sensitive and intelligent woman. It, alone, would be enough to undo the average person. But Anne had the added distress of being exposed to the public in a very intrusive manner. With the whirlwind of events following the death of *The Little Eaglet*, as the press had so unkindly dubbed their child, the Lindberghs had their faith in humanity shaken to its core. The Lindberghs' second child, Jon, was traumatized, when his nurse was forced off the road by another car, while driving him to nursery school one morning. Cameras were poked at the frightened child. Pictures of Jon appeared in newspapers the following morning. Anne withdrew him from school.

Fearful for their safety and convinced that they were not safe in the United States, Anne and her husband fled the country aboard a passenger ship to live in England. They lived on the run, moving from one short-term home, to the next: France, Switzerland and Hawaii. Each move illustrated their desperate attempts to insulate themselves from the ever-present *paparazzi* of that day.

They found peace in the air; Anne became a gifted pilot in her own right. She had become more spiritually reflective after the catastrophic death of their child. Poetic, by nature, she was also profoundly inspired by their flying experiences and kept detailed journals that became the basis of many of her poems and stories. Anne's achievement as co-pilot and radio operator for a geographical survey, which she and Charles had completed, was significant. In 1934 the National Geographic Society awarded her the Hubbard Gold Medal for distinction in exploration, research and discovery. She was the first woman to receive this medal.

> *"...To grow, to be reborn, one must remain vulnerable and open to love, but also hideously open to the possibility of more suffering."*

In 1936 the need to know more about Germany's military power became apparent. As an aviation expert was needed, Major Truman Smith, attaché to the American Embassy in Berlin, wrote to Charles and invited him to take on the task. He accepted. Anne accompanied him, and it was during one of their visits that information was divulged to Charles that Germany was building more army planes than American Intelligence was aware of. In 1938 Anne and Charles attended a banquet where, Herman Goering, flattered that the world-famous Lindbergh was his guest, presented him with a medal honoring him for his achievements in aviation and for being the first man to fly the Atlantic.

The press began to attack the Lindberghs. There were widespread rumors. One of Anne's books, *Listen! The Wind* was banned. Angered, Charles resigned from the Army Air Corps. Ten years earlier Anne had shared in public adoration of her husband. Now she shared in attacks on his integrity. History will be the judge.

After the war, Anne and Charles bought a home in Connecticut and, with their family, lived a quiet life. In the summer, they hiked, bicycled, and swam; during the winter, they skied, listened to music and read around the warmth of the fireplace. They instilled in their children the importance of self-reliance. No doubt this was as a result of the difficulties they had experienced in the past.

...Anne wrote many books. Perhaps her most famous, and the one that describes her delicate probing mind best, was Gift from the Sea.

During the 1950s and 1960s Anne wrote many books. Perhaps her most famous, and the one that describes her delicate probing mind best, was *Gift from the Sea.* It was written on a retreat to the seashore to sort out her life as a wife and mother. The shells she found, as she combed the beach, helped her to reflect on different stages of her life. The final gift from the sea was a rare creature, the *Argonauta,* sometimes called the *Paper Nautilus,* which is not fastened to its shell at all. It is actually a cradle for the young, held in the arms of the mother argonauta, who floats with it to the surface, where the eggs hatch, and the young swim away. The mother leaves her shell to begin another new stage of life. And so, Anne, the mother whose children had gone to school or begun their careers, found a connection with this empty shell, for she, too, was no longer the center of attention, with other lives revolving around her. The theme of *Gift from the Sea* struck a cord with women. It became a best seller.

In the late 60s Anne and Charles became concerned about the earth's environment. Anne, who usually declined invitations to speak before groups, was troubled by the condition of the environment and, in February 1970, at her Alma Mater, Smith College, made a rare public speech about environmental pollution. She was awarded an honorary Doctor of Letters degree. Afterwards, Anne resumed her quiet, private life.

When doctors told Charles that he was dying of cancer, he asked Anne to have him flown to *Argonauta*, their home in Maui, named after the shell in Anne's book, *Gift from the Sea*. It was his favorite retreat. Two weeks later, on August 1, 1974, Charles died.

With the death of her husband, Anne found continuity in her life through her five children and twelve grandchildren, scattered over the world. Her love of writing never deserted her. For Anne, an experience was not over until it was written down. Her best works, notably, *Listen! The Wind, North to the Orient* and *Gift from the Sea*, ensure Anne a niche, however narrow, in American literature. She died at age 95, spending her final years compiling her husband's papers and preparing them for publication.

Anne realized that her marriage to Charles Lindbergh was somewhat of a mismatch. Charles was a man of action; Anne, a woman of thought. Charles was a public hero; Anne, a private person. She was somewhat lost in the shadow of her husband's fame. Yet, Anne Morrow Lindbergh, writer, aviator, conservationist, wife and mother, was a remarkable woman in her own right. Said Charles Lindbergh, "No woman exists or has existed who is her equal."

Look for These Traits in Anne's Handwriting

1. Self-Control: When the crossbar of the letter *t*, is bent into a dome-like bow, it implies a bending of the will and suggests that the writer is trying to overcome a habit.

2. Thinking, quick: Retraced, needle-like, upward-pointing strokes, usually found in *m*'s and *n*'s. The writer thinks quickly, seeming to reach conclusions almost instantly.

3. Thinking, analytical: V-shaped wedges at the baseline show a writer who has analytical ability—the capacity to evaluate information; the deeper the wedges, the more penetrating the analytical ability.

4. Intuition: Frequent breaks between cursive structures indicate quick and ready insight, the power to attain direct knowledge without rational thought or inference.

5. Artistic: Printed capitals that begin a proper noun or a sentence show a desire for simplicity and reflect artistic inclinations.

6. Directness: Letters, beginning with a simple initial down stroke, indicate directness. The writer gets to the point, without wasting time.

DEACON BROWN'S POINT
NORTH HAVEN
MAINE

Anne wrote this letter to her sister,
Constance, in the 1930s.

7. Determination: Heavy downstrokes, below the baseline, give evidence of determination; the width or heaviness indicates strength; the length indicates endurance. The writer can have firmness of purpose.

8. Emotional Response: The writing tends to be straight up and down, showing objectivity. The head rules the feelings.

9. Cultural Desires: A Greek *e*, which can be seen in the formation of the letter *e*, indicates a desire for culture. This letter structure may appear in other letters, such as *r*. The writer desires refinement of thought, emotions, manners and taste.

What Handwriting Reveals About Anne

THE ABILITY TO control one's self rarely comes by inheritance. Anne had learned to control her will. When the will is bent, no task is too difficult. We see this in the dome-like shape of *t* crossings in Anne's writing. Having set her course, she would follow through with strong determination to finish a task. This is indicated in the long, strong downstrokes of Anne's writing; the stroke becomes heavier at the end showing the ability to dig down deep to finish an undertaking.

Her intuitiveness is a prime factor in her creative personality, a strong contributor to talent.

Anne was gifted with a marked insight that enabled her to understand and interpret, without effort or conscious reasoning. The breaks in her writing are so consistent that it often looks like printing. Her intuitiveness is a prime factor in her creative personality, a strong contributor to talent. She was able to adjust quickly to changing situations, seen in the needlelike points of her *m*'s and *n*'s. Anne had a strong, alert and positive personality. She also had a strong ability to analyze, seen in the wedges at the base of many of the letters in her writing. Anne could very well be classified as brilliant. The heaviness of her script adds depth to her thoughts; she was affected by what she heard, smelled, touched and felt.

Directness is indicated in handwriting when there is no approach stroke to a letter formation. The writer goes directly to the issue, be it intellectual or practical. Anne had few approach strokes, which added greatly to her accomplishments. She could not be bothered with the soup and salad, but went directly to the meat and potatoes of a subject

The Greek *e*'s, seen throughout Anne's writing, indicate a refined delicacy and sense of good taste. She appreciated the finer things of life. She would want her home to be uncluttered, full of music, beauty and space.

As we look at Anne Morrow Lindbergh, writer of beautiful thoughts, we might expect to find many loops in her handwriting, indicating a strong imagination; such is not the case. Her original thoughts were not the result of comparing them with some past experience, but rather from her own, intuitive insightfulness. In her case her imagination would have gotten in the way of these original thoughts.

The Greek *e*'s, seen throughout Anne's writing, indicate a refined delicacy and sense of good taste.

A.J. Cronin said, "The virtue of all achievement is victory over one's self." *Victory over one's self* was not only seen in her handwriting, but also manifested itself in her life, as the daughter of an Ambassador, wife of an American Hero and mother of a large family. She lived through the Lindbergh kidnapping and its aftermath, never losing her feeling of self-worth. With quiet, good taste, Anne left her own mark in life as a writer, pilot and environmentalist.

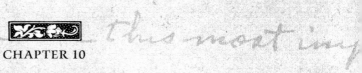

CHAPTER 10

GOLDA MEIR

1898–1978

Golda Meir

Handwriting...expresses the real you—your ambitions, fan-
tasies, goals, talents...what you are and what you might have
been—and clues to what you "still" can be.

NADYA OLYANOVA, RUSSIAN/AMERICAN GRAPHOLOGIST

AND AUTHOR, *The Psychology of Handwriting*, 1981

THE MABOVITCHS, OF Kiev, Russia, agreed that Golda was the most obstinate child in their family. Reasoning, shouting, even spanking just did not work. When Golda made up her mind, it stayed made up.

As a child Golda and her family lived with other Jews in *The Pale of Settlement*. She recalled the frightening experiences of the *pogroms* in the late 1800s, ordered by the Czar to divert revolutionary anger to the masses. His select soldiers, the Cossacks, would race through parts of the settlement on horseback, raiding and pillaging, often killing Jews in the process. This left an indelible print on little Golda Mabovitch's mind.

Golda's mother decided that things were getting too dangerous for them. She decided to take the family to America to reunite with Golda's father, who had immigrated earlier to find a better life for the family. What a thrill it was to see Moshe waiting for them at the train station in Milwaukee.

It was a memorable day for Golda when, at her Milwaukee elementary school, she memorized and repeated these words: "I pledge allegiance to the flag...with liberty and justice for all." What beautiful words to a little girl who, at eight years of age, had already experienced too many injustices in her young life; these words filled Golda with awe. If she could have looked into the future, she would have had an even greater feeling of awe, for, on a warm day in May 1948, she would sign her name to a declaration, much like the Declaration of Independence; by so doing she would help to found the new country of Israel.

As Golda matured she began speaking out publicly regarding injustices toward Jews. She was incensed, because her kinsmen, in Europe, could not practice their religion, their traditions or their cherished way of life. When Golda heard David Ben Gurion speak about the new nation of Israel, she returned home to tell her family and her fiancé, Morris Meyerson, about some revolutionary new ideas. When Golda told them that she was willing to go to Palestine and live in a kibbutz, they were dumbfounded. More and more, Golda's thoughts turned toward the political theory of Zionism and plans for building a homeland for Jews in Palestine.

Jewish history goes back to the descendants of the tribes of Israel. The patriarchs, Abraham, Isaac and Jacob, considered the land of Canaan their home. The ancient history of the Jewish people continues with their settlement in Egypt. After an Exodus from Egypt, the tribes of Israel conquered Canaan. This ancient land of Canaan would today encompass Israel, the West Bank, The Gaza Strip, Jordan and the southern portions of Syria and Lebanon. Throughout time many names have been given this area including Palestine and the Holy Land. The earliest known name was Canaan.

In November 1917 a National Home for Jewish People was established in Palestine. Golda and Morris were married the same year. They began scrimping and saving and, after four years, had enough money for their voyage. The great adventure was about to begin. The year was 1921. Golda, Morris and the friends she had inspired to join them were on their way.

She was so dedicated to this cause that, when they sailed from Italy on the final leg of their journey to Jerusalem, Golda surrendered her beloved American passport; she was burning her bridges behind her. She changed her name from Meyerson to the Jewish Meir.

Most people in the kibbutzim were from poor European countries. They jeered at the spoiled Americans, saying they would never make the grade. Golda prevailed and, though often dead tired, always persevered. Slowly, her body began to toughen; she began to gain respect from the other kibbutzniks. Golda's talent, as a leader, became apparent. She was asked to assume one position after another.

In 1938 Golda, representing Palestine, attended an international conference to study the problem of Hitler's imprisonment of millions of Jews in concentration camps. One country after another gave its sympathy, but no help. The United States agreed to take 27,000 Jews, per year, as immigrants. Golda's thoughts turned to millions of other Jews; were they to be forgotten?

She held a press conference. The sad-looking, work-worn face of this forty-year-old woman, who undauntingly represented millions of Jews, struck the hearts of reporters attending the conference. The voice of Golda

Meir was being heard, and the cause of the Jewish citizens of the world was being broadcast. When World War II came to an end, the Nazis had killed six million Jews, one million of them children. What about those who had somehow survived? Most of them were displaced persons. They longed to go to Palestine, the *Promised Land*. Golda would do anything to help.

An Anglo-American Commission was finally formed and, in 1946, issued a report. 100,000 refugees would be admitted to Palestine immediately. The British were given the job of guiding the Jews to Statehood. In so doing they would allow only 2,000 Jews, per year, into Palestine, until the 100,000 were met.

When the Jews heard this, Jewish Palestine exploded. On June 14, 1946, every bridge, railroad track and road that crossed the borders of Palestine was blown up. The act was symbolic and achieved its effect on the world. The British were infuriated. They jailed most of the Jewish leaders—except Golda—she was too well-known. It was a stroke of good fortune, for she became the negotiator with the British and the Arabs of Palestine. And what a negotiator she was. The United Nations decided that there would be two nations, one for the Jews and one for the Arabs.

They jailed most of the Jewish leaders—except Golda—she was too well-known. It was a stroke of good fortune, for she became the negotiator with the British and the Arabs of Palestine.

In May 1948 Israel signed a Proclamation of Independence. At long last Israel was a nation, and Golda was there to sign this famous document. For six months the British remained as peacekeepers between the two nations. When they left, rioting and terror reigned. The Arab nation declared war on the Jews.

They must fight, but with what? Golda headed for the US on a fundraising campaign. She told her story time and again. It was said that, when she prepared tea for an intimate group of wealthy Jews, she refused their insistent requests to help her clean up after the tea until, finally they said, "But what can we do for you Golda?" "You can buy two jet planes for Israel." She shot back with a twinkle in her eye—she got the planes.

Jewish leaders in America commented, "We had never seen anyone like her, so plain, so strong, so old fashioned. Just like a woman out of the Bible." As a guest on a radio talk show, while asking for funds, she also gave her recipe for chicken soup. 40,000 requests for her recipe were the result. She had a way of captivating her audiences. The miracle of her fundraising was repeated again and again, as she traveled through America. She was a consummate fundraiser, raising 50 million dollars in her campaign. Ben Gurion said: "One day it will be said that there was a Jewish woman who got the money which made the nation possible." And the Jews fought tooth and nail with the equipment Golda made possible.

> *Ben Gurion said: "One day it will be said that there was a Jewish woman who got the money which made the nation possible."*

In the following years, Golda saw the nation of Israel continue to grow. Immigrants were arriving at 1,000 a day: Jews from India, Jews from the Pampas of South America; Jews from every nation were returning home.

The 1960s were a time of extremely high tension between Israel and its Arab neighbors. During the six-day war in 1967, Israel had captured much Arab territory. Small battles continued to erupt.

Every post of the Israel government had been touched or influenced by Golda. In 1969, as a foreign delegate to Russia, it was a natural step for her to become Prime Minister, the first woman to hold the position in Israel. After her election, the tensions continued with the Arabs. Golda wanted to find peace, but she refused to back down to threats.

Just before dawn on October 6, 1973, Egypt and Syria made a surprise attack on Israel. Golda rallied the Israel forces which repelled the aggressors, penetrating deeply into Syrian and Egyptian territories. Many Israeli losses were sustained.

Although Israel did not lose ground, Golda was criticized by many Israelites for being unprepared for the attack. Her popularity dropped; she resigned several months later. This was a great personal tragedy for Golda. Yet, in spite of the difficulties confronting Israel, in the years that followed Golda's optimism never waned.

She had been quietly suffering with cancer for a number of years and, on Friday, December 8, 1978, Golda lost her fight. She had no taste for frills and wanted a simple funeral: no memorial and no eulogies. Her wishes were granted. But her greatness would not be forgotten. A snakelike line of 100,000 people stretched a half mile, to mourn and pay tribute to this great Jewish lady. Statesmen and leaders of many nations, as well as simple Kibbutzniks, were there. Her name had become intertwined with the history of the Jewish people and the world. Golda Meir was a grandmother and an international stateswoman, who held policy discussions over a cup of coffee in her kitchen. A leader of the Zionist movement, Golda worked untiringly for her cause.

The New York Times editorial best described her when it said, "The miracle of Golda Meir was how one person could perfectly embody the spirit of so many."

Look for These Traits in Golda's Handwriting

1. Directness: When letters begin with a simple initial downstroke, directness and simplicity are indicated.

2. Broad-Mindedness: ell-rounded e's, indicate broadmindness or tolerance of the views of others.

3. Unyielding: When a letter formation is firm and pointed, as in the letter *s*, the writer is unyielding. The writer will not be susceptible to influence or easily swayed.

4. Space: The greater the space between words, the more the writer needs his or her private space. This enables the writer to think clearly.

5. Thinking, independent: If the *t*- and *d*-stems are short in proportion to the rest of the writing, there is evidence of independent thinking. The writer is not bound to custom, but will act on his or her conclusions (see dictionary).

6. Initiative: When an upstroke above the base line, such as in the letter *h*, sharply leaps forward from the preceding downstroke, the writer shows initiative. The writer is able to spot opportunities.

Golda's writing is a note written in Vancouver, Canada, to Bernard Simpson in 1977.

7. Diplomacy: When writing tapers in size in a letter formation especially in the letter *m* or *n*, diplomacy is apparent. The writer will be tactful in dealing with people.

8. Emotional Response: The slant of the writing varies throughout Golda's writing.

9. Determination: Heavy downstrokes below the baseline are evidence of determination. The writer is inclined to be resolute or have a firmness of purpose.

10. Concentration: Small writing in lower case letters is seen throughout the writing, indicating the ability to focus.

What Handwriting Reveals About Golda

A REALISTIC DESCRIPTION of Golda Meir would begin with the fact that she was not glamorous, nor did she seek fame or recognition. Ego was not an issue with her and, as a result, her handwriting was not large or imposing. Only one thing mattered in Golda's life: That a nation could be created for the Jewish people.

The slant in Golda's writing, which varies from straight up and down to far forward, shows that she could be objective, but when her heart was appealed to, she would respond. She wanted the rights and desires of others to be recognized, especially those of her fellow Jews. She would not only respond, but would be open, broadminded and empathetic, which deepened her personal relationships. This is seen in the lower case e's,

Golda could *stand by her guns*...The points of the *s*'s, in her writing, give us a clue that she would not yield in her resolve.

which allowed her to open herself to the needs of others, helping her to adjust quickly, accept advice and deal with people understandably and sympathetically. However, it should be noted that Golda could *stand by her guns*...The points of the *s*'s, in her writing, give us a clue that she would not yield in her resolve. These qualities were a driving force that carried Golda over formidable obstacles.

Golda showed clarity of thinking, seen in well-spaced words, such as in the third line between *in* and *making*. The closely dotted *i*'s of Golda's writing, seen in the words *is* and *Justice*, indicate that no details would be overlooked. She would stick with a project until its completion, ignoring intrusions.

Golda was able to form her own conclusions, revealed in the short-stemmed *t*'s and *d*'s of her writing. She respected the opinions of others, yet reserved the right to make up her own mind in her own way. Because she could focus, shown in the smallness of her lower case letters, she would not waste energy, making tremendous work output possible.

She had the ability to be direct, to come straight to the point, seen in the absence of approach strokes in her writing. Golda wanted no small talk and would have seemed abrupt had it not been for the softening quality of diplomacy, revealed in the downward slant of the capital M's in *Miriam* and *Meir*. She had the quality of being able to deal with others without friction. She could communicate with kibbutznicks, yet shine in her negotiation with world powers.

She was a self-starter. This is revealed in the breakaway strokes of the *h*'s.

When the going was rough, as it so often was in Golda's life, she would move forward, initiating new ideas and actions. She was a self-starter. This is revealed in the breakaway strokes of the *h*'s. Adding to this, she had staying power, finishing the task regardless of interruptions, as indicated in the heavy downward strokes in such letters as *y* and *g*.

To summarize we see spaces between letters and words, giving her clarity of thought and a heart that was open. Golda was known for both her toughness and her warm personality. She was diplomatic, genuine, and empathetic. She knew where she was going—and why.

CHAPTER 11

MARIA MONTESSORI

1870–1952

Maria Montessori

The moving finger writes and having writ moves on:

Not all your piety or your wit shall lure it back to cancel half

a line, nor all your tears wash out a word of it.

The Rubaiyat, OMAR KHAYYAM,

POET AND MATHEMATICIAN, ELEVENTH CENTURY

MARIA MONTESSORI WAS born near Ancona, an Adriatic seaport in Italy. She was the only child of Renilde Stoppani, an educated woman from a well-off family, and Alessandro Montessori, an army officer, turned civil servant. Little did this child from an ordinary Italian family realize that one day she would be acknowledged as not only one of the world's leading educators, but also a strong advocate for peace. She was an individual who was ahead of her time.

Maria was an outspoken, independent-minded child who was usually the leader in games with other children at school. Maria, as a young girl, disregarding opposition from her father and teachers, insisted that she be allowed to attend classes in mathematics and science at an all-boys technical school. With the study of mathematics, she became interested in engineering, but eventually focused on biology and began thinking about medicine.

Her parents wanted her to become a teacher, but she had sworn that she would never be a teacher which, at that time, was one of only a few careers outside marriage considered suitable for women. In time Maria did something never attempted by a woman before. She presented herself at the gates of the medical school of the University of Rome and, in 1896, was the first Italian woman to receive a medical degree.

As a physician, Dr. Montessori specialized in pediatrics and psychiatry. She taught at the medical school and, through its free clinics, came into frequent contact with children of the working class and the poor.

She realized, as she worked with these children, that they had a spontaneous interest in learning. She began by working with the slow learners and found that they learned best by seeing, hearing, touching, tasting and smelling, always at their own pace. It became apparent to Dr. Montessori that children paced their own development through sensitive periods in their lives. Indeed, she found that the first thing a child should learn is the difference between order and disorder. It was from such basic concepts that the Montessori Method of teaching developed, always recognizing the uniqueness of each child. She believed that a child is a unique, irreplaceable and priceless gift from God, not just a piece of property.

In studying retarded children, Maria would listen carefully, noting everything they said and did. Slowly, she began to get a sense of who they really were; in turn, the children became acutely aware of their own senses, their language and society.

Although Maria began as a doctor, fate had intervened. In spite of her initial dread of becoming a teacher, reality prevailed; she found her true vocation.

Her success with children and their disabilities inspired her to adapt her methods to the education of children without disabilities and, in 1907, she opened the first Casa Dei Bambini (Children's House) in the slums of Rome.

As the name suggests, The Casa Dei Bambini was a house for children, rather than a real school. It was a place where a diffused culture could be assimilated, without any need for direct instruction. The teacher's task was not to talk, but to prepare a series of cultural activities, made for the child in a special environment.

She believed that a child is a unique, irreplaceable and priceless gift from God, not just a piece of property.

The final test of the child's reaction to this kind of setting came shortly after the school became famous. A group of well-intentioned women gave the school a marvelous collection of lovely, expensive toys. These toys proved to be a temporary attraction that held the children's attention for a few days; they soon returned to the more interesting learning materials. Children do advanced mathematics in Montessori schools, not because they are pushed, but because this is what they do when given the correct setting and opportunity.

As the news of her schools spread, she began to accept speaking engagements throughout Europe. So brilliant was her mind that she never wrote her oral presentations, nor did she give the same speech twice. Her delivery was flawless, her themes exceptional. The truth is that when Maria spoke, she did so with great simplicity, never suggesting how complex her ideas really were.

Maria could also be full of fun. Margot Waltuch, her interpreter, tells of an occasion when, in the middle of a lecture, Maria motioned for Margot to come over and whispered to her, "I must be brilliant today. Look down in the fourth row, left seat." There was a man snoring, sound asleep.

Many of the puzzles and educational devices, now in use at the pre-school and elementary levels of education, are direct copies of Montessori's original ideas.

Those who studied under her and went on to make their own contributions to education and child psychology include Anna Freud and Alfred Adler. Montessori schools have taken root all over the world—in Europe, the Americas, Russia, India, China and Japan. Maria Montessori caused a revolution in the classroom. Even the physical aspect of elementary schoolrooms changed from dull regimentation to colorful informality. Many of the puzzles and educational devices, now in use at the pre-school and elementary levels of education, are direct copies of Montessori's original ideas.

As the name *Montessori Education* was never copyrighted, the right of anyone to use the name Montessori, as a school or method, became widespread. Few Montessori schools have teachers trained in the true *Montessori Method*.

During her lifetime, Dr. Montessori was acknowledged as one of the world's leading educators. She is as controversial a figure in education, today, as she was a half a century ago. Alternately heralded as the century's leading advocate for early childhood education or, dismissed as outdated and irrelevant, her research and the studies she developed have helped change the course of education. Only recently, as our understanding of child development has grown, have we rediscovered how clear and sensible her insights were.

Maria Montessori's career extended beyond the goals of learning and the concerns of teachers and parents. She was a great advocate for peace and was responsible for two International Congresses on peace. Her tombstone in Noorwijk, Holland states, "I ask the dear, all powerful children, to unite with me for the building of peace in man and in the world."

Look for These Traits in Maria's Handwriting

1. Emotional Response: The slant of the upstrokes of handwriting indicates the range, frequency and intensity of a writer's internal, emotional responses. Far-forward slant writers usually act quickly (see dictionary).

2. Unyielding: When a writer has firm lower case letters such as a pointed *s*, she will not easily yield to the influence of others.

3. Caution: When words end with a straight final stroke usually at the end of a line, caution is indicated. The cautious writer is reluctant to rush into situations or act rashly.

Maria's handwriting is a sample from The Association Montessori Internationale, The Netherlands.

4. Thinking, quick: Needle-like retracing of *m*'s and *n*'s indicate an instant grasp of subjects.

5. Rhythm: The regular return of the writing to the baseline or, writing with a beat, suggests that the individual possesses the quality of rhythm. The writer thinks and moves in an orderly manner. This trait affects all other traits.

6. Thinking, analytical: When *v*-shaped wedges come down to the base-line, the writer shows analytical ability.

7. Emotional Depth: Heaviness of writing is seen throughout Maria's writing. It implies how deeply an emotional situation will affect the writer (see dictionary).

8. Diplomacy: When writing tapers toward the end of a letter formation, especially in the *m* and *n*, the writer is diplomatic and will be tactful in dealing with people.

What Handwriting Reveals About Maria

OUR EMOTIONAL FOUNDATION is made up of how quickly and deeply we respond in any given situation. This is shown in the slant and depth of the writing.

Maria Montessori's handwriting has the qualities of a highly responsive individual, seen in the far-forward slant of her writing. Emotional depth, indicated by the heaviness of the line of writing, is something different. It can be the most powerful element in human personality. When her heart was appealed to, she responded quickly and deeply. A build-up of ink at the beginning of certain strokes would add to this intense feeling

We see in the sharp wedges in her *m*'s and *n*'s the ability to delve into subjects and then analyze in an incisive manner. Added to this are the needle-like points in such strokes as the small *m* of *Bambino*, indicating that she was able to pick up information very quickly, as her mind traveled from one subject to another. She was mentally alert and had a strong need to find her own answers; she could even go so far as resenting people who tried to do her thinking for her.

Caution is often thought of as holding one back but, in Maria's case, it could be an asset. If nothing else, it gave others time to catch up with her rapid thinking processes.

To minimize, somewhat, her highly emotional nature, she developed caution, clearly seen in the final stroke of several of her words. She was constantly putting a check on her tendency to rush forward impulsively or rashly. Caution is often thought of as holding one back but, in Maria's case, it could be an asset. If nothing else, it gave others time to catch up with her rapid thinking processes.

Maria had a rare combination of traits in her handwriting. The points of the *s* in Montessori show us that she was unyielding; she would stand her ground on an issue, never budging on her principles. Yet, she could be diplomatic, seen in the diminishing capital *M*'s in her signature. Strong convictions and diplomacy formed a fine combination for Maria, when dealing with people.

Maria's handwriting returns to the baseline in a very rhythmic fashion and with a sense of uniform timing. This gave her a natural flow of thoughts that enhanced her mobility in any venture. This orderly pattern added style to what she said or did.

Strong convictions and diplomacy formed a fine combination for Maria, when dealing with people.

She had the potential to strongly move people, not only with words, but with her eyes, the tone of her voice, her gestures and movements. She was a spark-plug. This power could be put to use in politics, motivational speaking and, in Maria's case, as a renowned teacher and charismatic leader. The emotionally responsive writing that slants strongly to the right tells us this. Her keen mind and unyielding personality drove her forward. We see this in her life and in her handwriting.

CHAPTER 12

LUCY MAUD MONTGOMERY MACDONALD

1874–1942

L. M. Montgomery Macdonald
1929

Conscious handwriting is an unconscious drawing.

MAX PULVER, SWISS PSYCHOLOGIST, THE 1940s

ANNE SHIRLEY, THE imaginative, red-haired orphan and protagonist of the story, *Anne of Green Gables*, was always on the lookout for "kindred spirits and exploring the mysteries of life." Mark Twain pronounced her "The dearest and most lovable child in fiction since the immortal Alice."

Most of us are familiar with the story of *Anne of Green Gables*, but very few know Lucy Maud Montgomery, the author of the famous book. Maud, as she liked to be called, was born on Prince Edward Island, just off the northeastern coast of mainland Canada; the island curves into the opening of the Gulf of St. Lawrence. She had a storyteller's gift and was earning money from her pen by the early 1900s. Her talent was to weave the threads of her life—her Scots blood, her life on Prince Edward Island and her experiences as a teacher—into charming literary classics.

At age two, her grandparents took her to live with them in Cavendish, Prince Edward Island. Her mother had died of tuberculosis, and her father could no longer care for her. The Cavendish home had a strict atmosphere, both hard and cold. This environment was not easy for the imaginative, sensitive and temperamental Maud. She compensated for this with her avid love of reading and the writing of prose and poetry; Maud used her vivid imagination to take her out of her isolation. She struggled alone; most of her relatives thought her *scribbling* was foolish.

She attended a small, white-washed school across the road from her grandparents' home. She remembers in her diary: "I shall always be thankful that my school was near a grove—a place with winding paths and treasure-troves of mosses and wood-flowers...a stronger and better educative influence in my life than the lessons learned at the desk of the schoolhouse...Were it not for those Cavendish years, I do not think *Anne of Green Gables* would have been written."

The stirring of lovely ideas, even before she had the vocabulary to express these thoughts, shows itself in some excerpts from her autobiography. In one she recalls a little fern growing in the forest and, in another, a shallow sheet of June Bells under the firs. Her autobiography states her love of writing very clearly. "I cannot remember the time when I was not writing or when I did not mean to be an author. To write has always been my central purpose around which every effect, hope and ambition of my life has grouped itself..." Writing about imaginary characters was her escape from her earliest childhood.

When Maud was twelve, she recited a poem. Someone commented, "The words were very pretty." Maud was so thrilled that she ran out of the house, holding those sweet words in her heart. The house was not big enough to contain her joy; she needed the whole of the outdoors.

Upon completion of her elementary education, she began to study for the entrance examination at Prince Wales College and, in 1893, Maud entered the college and successfully completed the program required for a teacher's license. She taught for four years. "During those winters of school teaching...I got up at 6 o'clock and dressed by lamplight...I would put on a heavy coat, sit on my feet to keep them from freezing, with my fingers so cramped that I could scarcely hold the pen...I would write my *stunt* for the day."

Prince Edward Islanders were known to be loyal, clannish, upright and hardworking. These solid and strong traits were very much a part of Maud and she lived by them. When her grandfather died in 1898, Maud immediately resigned her teaching position and returned to Cavendish to live with her grandmother. She had promised her grandmother that she would never leave her. Maud spent most of the next thirteen years assisting her grandmother as postmistress of the little post office attached to their home.

Throughout all these years, she continued to write short stories for serials in magazines in Canada and the United States, so much so that she was able to make a livable income by her pen. At age thirty-one, Maud began the story of *Anne of Green Gables*, sending it off to many publishers and receiving as many rejections. She hid the story away.

A quote from Maud's memoirs shows us how fate intervened. "The manuscript lay in the hatbox until I came across it one winter day while rummaging. I began turning over the leaves, reading a bit here and there. It didn't seem so very bad. 'I'll try once more,' I thought..." It was finally accepted and was to be her best publication...*Anne of Green Gables*.

The popularity of her book was immense. She received hundreds of letters from all over the world, often addressed to Miss Anne Shirley, Green Gables, Avonlea, Prince Edward Island. The themes, tone and style of her stories had created a worldwide circle of devotees.

She remained true to the promise made to her grandmother that she would never leave her, even though she had been secretly engaged since 1906, to Ewan MacDonald, a Presbyterian minister. When her grandmother died in March 1911, Maud immediately made plans for her marriage to Ewan. She thought him a good *catch* and a respected member of the community.

Ewan and Maud were married in July 1911. After a two-month honeymoon on the British Isles, they returned to live in Leaksdale, Ontario, where they raised two sons. The adjustment to life outside her beloved Prince Edward Island was difficult for Maud. She stated that, no matter how difficult things were, no matter how she felt about certain people or conditions of her life, she would be cheerful and outgoing.

> *I began turning over the leaves, reading a bit here and there. It didn't seem so very bad. 'I'll try once more' I thought"....It was finally accepted and was to be her best publication...*Anne of Green Gables.

Maud was an indefatigable letter writer. Mollie Gillen, in her biography, *The Wheel of Things,* states that Maud corresponded with many individuals. She began a correspondence with two men, both of whom she had met only briefly. These communications lasted for forty-odd of her sixty-seven years. It was through Gillen's sleuthing that these letters were found and brought to light. They revealed much about her life that otherwise would have remained hidden.

Maud was an avid scrapbook keeper. She spoke with nostalgia about her scrapbooks that were filled with memorabilia from her life. She loved pussycats. In Maud's autobiography, *The Alpine Path*, she said, "I had two pet kittens, Catkin and Pussy-willow. Catkin was a little too meek and pink-nosed to suit me, but Pussy-willow was the prettiest, *cutest* little scrap of gray-striped fur ever seen, and I loved her passionately." Many pictures of these little animal *friends* were in her scrapbooks. Her signature, with a small kitten drawn near the underscore, became her trademark.

A woman's ability to be creative and artistically inclined was often questioned. Surprisingly, her books became best sellers.

Ewan was transferred to Toronto, Ontario, where they lived until 1935. These were difficult years for Maud. Her husband was seriously ill. He suffered from great bouts of depression. There was no known treatment for his illness. Maud always held up a good front for the world, but often felt very alone and starved for companion-ship. To compensate, as she had done as a child, she would return to her writing for solace.

Maud lived in an era when being a woman writer was not always acceptable. A woman's ability to be creative and artistically inclined was often questioned. Surprisingly, her books became best sellers. Although she was scorned by aca-demic critics, she continued to write successfully. Her amazing success encouraged her to continue. The additional income was welcomed because of Ewan's limited means as a parson and his illness. Both Ewan and Maud were under doctor's care the last years of their lives. She died in 1942 at age 67. Ewan died five years later and was buried beside her in Cavendish, on a hill overlooking the land and sea that she loved.

At her death she left 10 volumes (over 5000 pages) of unpublished per-sonal diaries. During her lifetime she published 22 books of fiction, 450 poems and 500 short stories.

In 1923 Lucy Maud Montgomery MacDonald became the first Canadian woman to be made a fellow of the Royal Society of Arts in Great Britain. In 1935 she was made an officer of the Order of the British Empire. The Canadian government purchased land in Cavendish, on Prince Edward Island, which was designated a National Park in honor of Maud.

Her ear for dialogue, together with her insight into human nature and her choice of themes, has made her Canada's enduring literary export, and red-haired *Anne* has become a world-famous literary character.

Look for These Traits in Maud's Handwriting

Maud's handwriting comes from a page of her diary (date unknown).

Maud's love of kittens shows up in the little cat-symbols she often used with her signature.

1. Thinking, independent: When *d-* or *t*–stems are short in relation to the height of the lower case letters, there is evidence of independence. The writer is not bound to custom, but will act on his or her own conclusions.

2. Thinking, quick: Retraced needle-like upward strokes usually found in *m*'s and *n*'s. The writer thinks quickly, seeming to reach conclusions almost instantly.

3. Yieldingness: A soft or rounded structure, particularly in the *s*, implies a yielding nature. The writer is susceptible to influence.

4. Goals: The crossbar of the letter *t* illustrates where the writer places his or her goals in life. Maud's *t*'s are crossed at the top, giving her high goals (see dictionary).

5. Worry: When the downstroke of an *m* or *n* makes a loop on its return there is an indication of unrealistic imagination. The writer can become anxious, distressed or uneasy. This is often seen in the capital letter *M*.

6. Secretive / Self-Deceit: Loops in circle letters indicate self deception and secretiveness (see dictionary).

7. Fluidity: Strokes that flow into one another often seen as a figure eight in an *f* or *g* indicate fluidity in thought or action. It is implied that the writer expresses him or herself with ease.

8. Broad-Mindedness: Well-rounded, circle letters *a, e, d, g, q* and *o* imply broadmindedness, or tolerance of the views of others.

What Handwriting Reveals About Maud

LUCY MAUD MONTGOMERY Macdonald's handwriting gives us a glimpse into her life and her personality. Her mind was always open to new ideas, seen in the open *e*'s of her writing. Once having perceived a new thought, she would immediately grasp its essence. The needlelike points on the tops of the letters *m* and *n,* show a quick mental acuity. She could immediately comprehend a subject, especially one with which she was familiar. Fluidity is seen in the letter *f* of *frost.* Because her thoughts flowed smoothly, she could record her thoughts, present her ideas and, with little effort weave the tales of Avonlea.

One cannot help but compare the independent spirit of the fictional Anne of Avonlea, and see the parallel as we look at Maud's independence in her handwriting.

Maud was inclined to think independently; she was not easily influenced by customs, opinions or prejudices. We see this especially in the short-stemmed *d*'s of her handwriting. It has been said that a reader may recognize an author's imprint in his or her work. One cannot help but compare the independent spirit of the fictional Anne of Avonlea and see the parallel as we look at Maud's independence in her handwriting.

Maud showed a certain amount of flexibility, the capacity to yield in certain situations, seen in the softening in many of the *s*'s in her writing. She was capable of adopting new courses and acting on them, which enhanced her chances for achievement. This tendency to yield can have a positive or negative effect. The positive effect could provide variety in her story telling, whereas the negative could cause her to give in to her own frailties.

She was not always honest with herself about certain unpleasant realities in her life, shown in the loops in her *a*'s and *o*'s. Added to this we found, in the loops of the upstrokes of the capital *M*'s, a strong capacity to worry, making Maud anxious, troubled and uneasy. In our research, we were not surprised to find that she was dejected and sad a good part of her life.

Fortunately, she was capable of rising above these difficulties. As we look more deeply into Maud's handwriting, we see high *t* crossings, showing us that she set long-range goals. Her goals were not only high, they were strong and forceful, seen in the heaviness of the *t*-crossing. She had strength and clarity of purpose. This helped to give her life a sense of direction.

> **As we look more deeply into Maud's handwriting, we see high *t* crossings, showing us that she set long-range goals.**

Her handwriting gives us a glimpse into the human side of Maud, with all its talents and frailties. Yet, despite her personal struggle, or possibly because of it, she was able to spin the tale of Avonlea and Anne Shirley into a beloved story of life in the early Twentieth Century on Prince Edward Island.

CHAPTER 13

GRANDMA MOSES

1860–1961

Grandma Moses,

Every written signature is a mirror of peculiarities, which are
characteristics of individuals.

Disputed and Forged Documents, J. NEWTON BAKER, LL.M., J.D., 1955

IN 1860 THE woman the world would know as Grandma Moses was born Anna Mary Robertson, in obscurity in the Village of Eagles Bridge, New York. In 1938 an amateur art collector *discovered* some of Anna's paintings in a shop window. At eighty years of age she had her first public success as an artist. When she died at age a hundred and one, her art had achieved international renown. The name Grandma Moses had become a household word.

As a child Anna loved to make paper dolls, dressing them in scraps of paper and coloring them with grape and blackberry juice. Sometimes her father would bring her a special present: sheets of blank newsprint. Anna got the most out of each sheet by covering every square inch with pencil and chalk drawings.

At age twelve Anna was ready to find employment and began to practice the skills she would one day need to run a farm household of her own. As there was little opportunity for a formal education, she *hired out,* as her mother had done before her. She could sew, clean house, garden, and tend to children. In her words she comments, "Then came the hard years."

> *...she hired out, as her mother had done before her. She could sew, clean house, garden and tend to children. In her words she comments, "Then came the hard years."*

It may have been while working on one of these farms that she saw Currier and Ives prints for the first time. These well-known lithograph drawings often depicted such activities as corn husking and maple sugaring. This may have been her first exposure to any formal art, an exposure that would have a lasting effect.

At age twenty-seven and unmarried, Anna was considered an *old maid.* She was in no hurry. She eventually met and married a young hired hand named Thomas Salmon Moses. In her words, "He found me a good cook, and I found him temperate and thrifty. In those days we didn't look for a man because he was rich, for that kind of *like* is not lasting, just lasts as long as the pocket book...I believed that we were a team, and that I had to do as much as my husband did."

The first of her ten children was born in 1888; five of these children died in infancy. Of the five, Grandma Moses noted sadly in her autobiography, "One lived to be six weeks and the others were dead born, *still born* they call it. I left five little graves in that beautiful Shenandoah Valley."

Grandma Moses' autobiography, *My Life Story,* speaks of the difficulties she faced as a pioneer woman. "...so I had four babies to care for. But we got along very nice 'til the children got the scarlet fever. That was a hard year, but it passed just like all the rest."

One is immediately struck by the fiber and strength of character running through this extraordinary woman, living a very ordinary life as a farm-woman in the late 1800s. She heroically held onto the good, while overlooking the difficult. Looking at her paintings, we are impressed by the lighthearted, happy and colorful depictions of the life she remembered from childhood.

Soon after her fifty-eighth birthday, Grandma Moses decided to wallpaper her living room. The work was going well until she came to the fire board, a wooden plank placed in front of the fireplace in the summer and ran out of paper. "So I took a piece of paper and pasted it over the board...I painted it a solid color first, then I painted two large trees on each side of it, like butternut trees. And back of it I did a little scene of a lake and painted it a yellow color, really bright, as though you were looking into the sunlight...I daubed it all on with a brush I painted the floor with." This episode exemplifies the practical way she approached life. She was not wasteful or extravagant, but pragmatic in her approach to life. The fireboard was restored and now hangs in the Grandma Moses Archive at the Galerie St. Etienne in New York.

Her first significant art sale was a request for ten paintings. Having only completed nine, she cut one in half and framed the two halves to provide ten for her customer.

She is remembered best for the details she lovingly and carefully put into each scene. She colored the world around her, as she remembered it from childhood: the fields, the farms, the sky, children on sleds and trees, brightly green or snow covered. These she saw through eyes that never lost their sense of childhood wonder.

> *She colored the world around her, as she remembered it from childhood: the fields, the farms, the sky, children on sleds and trees, brightly green or snow covered.*

Although the paintings themselves were simple, the effect conveyed ran much deeper, portraying the human longing for the joys of childhood and all that it means. This could well have been one of the reasons for the great popularity of her artwork.

Grandma Moses' paintings were as uncomplicated as her approach to life. What she painted required no interpretation: the children playing in the field, the turkey in the straw, the family gatherings; scenes that were just as she saw them.

With Grandma Moses' fame came the inevitable interviews, television appearances and the writing of her autobiography, *My Life's Story*. This story is clearly stated and done with complete sincerity. It was said that, when the legendary Edward R. Murrow, a veteran television host, was interviewing her, Grandma Moses did the interviewing. She simply overwhelmed people with her straightforwardness. The frankness and candor of Grandma Moses were like a breeze blowing through the haze of double talk, so often seen under these circumstances.

Grandma Moses rose above the hardships and embraced the joys of her life. Her remarkable life spanned twenty presidents. She remembered Lincoln's assassination and lived to see President Kennedy inaugurated. The spirit of women in America, in the late 1800s and early 1900s, was beauti-fully exemplified in the life of this extraordinary little woman who led an ordinary life until her eighties. She then began her life as a celebrity. Her *primitive* paintings, done from her childhood memories, now hang in the White House and in over twenty-nine major museums around the world. Her greatest gift was that she saw herself as she really was: a grandmother who had a gift for painting.

Look for These Traits in Grandma Moses' Handwriting

1. Thinking, independent: When the *d* and or *t* stems are short in relation to the height of the lower case letters, it is evidence of independent thinking. The writer is not bound to custom, but will act on his own conclusions (see dictionary).

2. Defiance: The buckle of the letter *k* should be in the lower case area. When it rises above this area, defiance is indicated, which is a resistance to authority or opposition.

3. Deliberateness: Separated stems, which are slightly rounded at the top, indicate a writer who is deliberate, prone to act more slowly in carrying out a task. The deliberate stroke is seen in the Moses writing in the separated stems of letters *m* and *n*.

4. Intuitive: Breaks between letter structures are evidence of intuition. It is assumed that the writer has the power to attain direct knowledge without rational thought or inference.

Then breakfast was ready and while we were eating Lester spied a little China dog on the clock shelf, and it was marked william Lester Robertson, so it was His,
then comenced the hunt for more toys, we found a small shepard dog on the reservoir, marked Horace Greely Robertson,
but so far nothing for me,
Then I found another little short legged dog marked arthur m, Robertson,
now as you know I felt pretty bad,
and mother said it was too bad as I had been a good girl; and for me to keep looking which I did,
when the men came in for dinner the hired man said he saw a lady lookling out of the window at him behind the ever greens, and sure nough There was little red ridinghood, for anna mary Robertson,
I could tell you a lot more about Christmas had I the time,

Grand ma moses,

Grandma Moses's handwriting is an excerpt from "Christmas."

5. Details, attention to: Closely dotted *i*'s is an indication that the writer pays close attention to details. The assumption is that people who pay close attention to details possess good memories.

6. Goals: *t*-bars, which are crossed three quarters of the way up the *t*-stems or higher indicate practical to high goals (see dictionary).

7. Argumentative: If the top of the first stroke in the letter *p* rises above the letter, the writer shows argumentativeness. The writer will want to discuss or debate an issue.

What Handwriting Reveals About Grandma Moses

THE QUALITIES IN the handwriting of this unusual little woman, which gave her the ability to move forward under difficult circumstances, are both strong and unique.

Grandma Moses was an independent person, shown in her short-stemmed *d*'s. She established her own rules and was unconcerned with what others thought of her. She could conform to a degree, but only if that conformity did not interfere with any of her principles.

Grandma Moses' greatest single asset, as a painter, was her close attention to detail. Her i's were precisely dotted.

Grandma Moses could dig in her heels. If her husband, Thomas Moses, could be interviewed today, he would likely say that Anna Mary would love and honor, but not necessarily obey. This is shown in the tall *k* of her writing, indicating a resistance to being told what to do. She could also be resolute in her opinions; the letter *p*, its height and construction, indicates this. She was a person who could be difficult to confront on certain issues. Softening these strong characteristics we see the slowly constructed letters of her writing, such as the deliberate stroke in the *m*'s.

The crossings of the *t*'s, in her script show that Grandma Moses had practical to high goals. Her handwriting shows a gentle optimism by the upward swing of the final strokes in her signature. She was strong in character, but gentle of spirit. Her thinking was slow and thoughtful, seen in the script of the *m*'s and *n*'s. These traits combined to give her a delicate cheerfulness.

Grandma Moses' greatest single asset, as a painter, was her close attention to detail. Her *i*'s were precisely dotted. As a result she could recall all her childhood memories in detail. This we see as we look at her paintings, remembering that she was 80 years old when she began to paint seriously.

We see breaks between letters within words of Grandma Moses' handwriting, giving her intuitive insight. This strongly influenced her interpretations of a given project and gave her the ability to add a deeper meaning to her *old time* art.

Her paintings show us the fond memories she had of her childhood and, in turn, provide us with a glimpse into Middle-America, in its pioneering days. Her handwriting, on the other hand, reveals insights into the stalwart personality of this artist and grandmother. Her stature was diminutive, but her talents were towering.

CHAPTER 14

MOTHER TERESA

1910–1997

Mother Teresa cradles an armless baby girl at her order's orphanage in Calcutta, India

God bless you
M Teresa mc

Spoken words are symbols of mental experience...Just as all
men do not have the same speech or sounds, neither
do they all have the same writing.

ARISTOTLE, GREEK PHILOSOPHER, 384–322 B.C.

AGNES GONXHA BOJAZHIU was born in Skopje, Albania. The Turkish Empire ruled Albania, and the majority of Albanians were Muslim. As devout Catholics, she and her family were in the minority.

In addition to her daily prayers and devotions, Agnes often read about the Croatian missionaries in India. When she was twelve she had a calling to become a missionary, but still wondered in her heart if this was her true path. She was advised to think and pray for guidance to make the right decision. She was still doubtful. Her confessor told her "Through your *joy* you will know. If you feel really happy by the idea that God is calling you, to serve him and your neighbor, that deep inner joy you feel is the compass that will indicate your direction in life."

Agnes decided to become a missionary and, at age 18, departed for a convent in Ireland, accompanied to the train station by the whole community of her small town: friends, schoolmates, neighbors, young and old, and, of course, her mother and sister. When she arrived in Dublin, she joined the Loretto Sisters, taking the name Teresa from Saint Teresa of Lisieux, *The Little Flower*.

"The most important journey of my life," she said, for it was on this trip that she became inspired to spend her life helping the poorest of poor.

Her first assignment was Calcutta, where she began studying to become a teacher. Crossing through the slums of Calcutta each day to reach her classroom, she became filled with compassion for the sick and starving, especially the children.

On September 10, 1946, she left by train for a retreat in Darjeeling in Northern India. "The most important journey of my life," she said, for it was on this trip that she became inspired to spend her life helping the poorest of poor. However, after thorough consideration, her Bishop refused permission. India was about to become independent and would no longer be a part of the British Empire. Sister Teresa was a European. There could be problems of a political nature. Would Rome approve this decision? Her Bishop told her she must wait.

In 1950, after much prayer and persistence, she received permission from Pope Pius XII to leave the Loretto Sisters and form her own community, which would be known as the Missionaries of Charity. After taking medical training to prepare for her new mission, she took her sisters into the slums of Calcutta to start a school for children. The children loved her and began calling her *Mother Teresa*.

> *After taking medical training to prepare for her new mission, she took her sisters into the slums of Calcutta to start a school for children. The children loved her and began calling her Mother Teresa.*

One can easily see how she was able to enroll others in her plans. She was a forward-looking person. "Unless life is lived for others, it is not worth living," she would say. Mother Teresa touched people from all walks of life, from royalty to convicted felons, from the very wealthy to the most destitute. She and Princess Diana spent many hours together. We were told that, when Diana was put to rest, clasped in her hands was a rosary given to her by Mother Teresa.

Through the years, Mother Teresa's fame grew, as did the magnitude of her deeds. "All people are our brothers and sisters," she often said. "Believers and non-believers have the opportunity, with us, to do works of love, the opportunity to share the joy of loving and come to realize God's presence."

"Hindus become better Hindus;
Catholics become better Catholics and
Muslims become better Muslims."

As she walked to an important meeting of dignitaries in Calcutta, Mother Teresa passed an open drain and caught sight of something moving. Upon investigation she found the remains of a dying man. She took him to a home where he could die in love and peace. "I lived like an animal in the streets," the man told her, "Now I will die like an angel." She did not go to the important meeting.

As she traveled the world people invariably asked her, "What can I do to help?" Mother Teresa's answer was always the same. "Just begin…begin at home…say something good to your child, your husband or your wife; begin helping someone in need in your community, at work or at school."

In 1979 the Norwegian Nobel Committee awarded Mother Teresa the Nobel Peace Prize, in recognition of her work in bringing help to suffering humanity and her respect for the worth and dignity of the individual human being.

In 1997, after years of reaching out to others with her whole heart and soul, giving totally, wholeheartedly, freely and unconditionally to the service of the poor, she went back to God.

She is best remembered for helping the desolate in India, which had always been her dream. Though she sought to avoid the spotlight, her humility and her work attracted attention and admiration. At the time of her death, her order of nuns had grown to more than 4,500 professed sisters in over 500 countries.

On October 19, 2003, Mother Teresa was beatified at St. Peter's Square. Over 200,000 people were there to bear witness to this first step toward the Canonization of Blessed Mother Teresa.

Look for These Traits in Mother Teresa's Handwriting

This is a copy of the original writing of Mother Teresa, procured for the author by a dear friend, Khmasea Bristol, in Cambodia in 1990.

MAKE US worthy, Lord to serve our fellow men throughout the world who live and die in poverty and hunger.
GIVE THEM, through our hands, this day their daily bread; and by our understanding love, give peace and joy.

PRINTED AS A GIFT TO THE MISSIONARIES OF CHARITY
BY THE KNIGHTS OF COLUMBUS

1. Diplomacy: When letters taper, in size, toward the end of a letter formation or word, the writer is diplomatic. In particular, he or she will be tactful in dealing with people.

2. Goals: The location of the *t*-bar above the *t*-stem indicates the goals of the writer (see dictionary). In the case of Mother Teresa, the goals would be considered visionary.

3. Optimism: Up-slanted *t*-bars, up-turned finals, and writing which has an inclined baseline, indicate optimism. The writer will be hopeful, looking on the bright side of things.

4. Intuition: Frequent breaks between cursive letters are evidence of intuitiveness. It is assumed that the writer has the power to attain direct knowledge, without rational thought or reference.

What Handwriting Reveals About Mother Teresa

MOTHER TERESA MAY have been diminutive in size and shy in personality, but her handwriting paints a different picture. The *t*-crossing that rises above the *t*-stem tells us Mother Teresa's goals were so far-reaching, that they could be considered visionary. The upward slant shows optimism.

It is interesting to note that her writing, rather than being squeezed, is open, with well-rounded letters, telling us that she made herself available to people. Mother Teresa was intuitive, seen in the breaks between letters. This enabled her to understand people and to interpret situations without effort. It also helped her to make the right decisions. The trait of diplomacy, which is helpful in relationships with people, is shown in the diminishing slant of the capital *M* and the *y* of the word *you*.

The *t*-crossing that rises above the *t*-stem tells us Mother Teresa's goals were so far-reaching, that they could be considered visionary.

As we look at Mother Teresa's handwriting, we see clear and simple letters. Clarity and simplicity echoed in her life and in the lives of the Sisters in her community. They lived in complete poverty, their worldly possessions being a habit and a small bucket for washing and carrying water.

Mother Teresa slept three to four hours a night and prayed five hours a day. Her definition of prayer was *shouting silently*. She shouted silently and the world heard. Though Mother Teresa's signature is limited in strokes, it gives us some strong insights into her life.

CHAPTER 15

FLORENCE NIGHTINGALE

1820–1910

MISS FLORENCE NIGHTINGALE.

Florence Nightingale.

I cannot help but think...that something of man's character

may be conjectured by his handwriting.

Chronicles of Canongate, SIR WALTER SCOTT,

SCOTTISH NOVELIST AND POET, 1771–1832

EW NAMES IN the ranks of outstanding women of history can produce the idyllic, noble, yet tender image that springs forth at the mention of the name Florence Nightingale, affectionately called, *The Lady with the Lamp.*

The legend of Florence Nightingale began as a result of two extraordinary events. In 1812 Florence's father, born William Shore, had succeeded to the estate of a relative, Peter Nightingale, a country squire. One condition was required: that he take the name Nightingale. Hence, William Edward Shore became William Nightingale.

William, with his inheritance and new name, married Francis Smith, a lady of privilege. Her father was a Member of Parliament. They spent much time abroad, often in Italy. It was during one of these visits, May 12, 1820, that a daughter was born to them in the beautiful city of Florence. Thus, the beloved English heroine came by her melodious name, Florence Nightingale.

A governess tutored Florence and her sister when they were young. When Florence was twelve, their father took over their education, teaching them classical languages, history and mathematics. It was far superior to the education of most girls of that day.

According to her diary, the turning point in Miss Nightingale's life occurred on February 7, 1837, when she received a *call from God* to a life of service. "My life is so filled with the misery of this world...my answer is to labor for and sympathize with the suffering..." Florence was depressed by the indifference of others.

For the first time she was seeing life as it really was, a stark contrast from her wealthy upbringing. To relieve the sufferings of others gave her life meaning. Florence had found a purpose in life. At this critical period in her life she decided to become a nurse, studying at a nursing institute in Germany. She then traveled to Paris, spending time with the Roman Catholic Sisters of St. Paul.

While there she studied surgery, comparing French Hospital systems and methods of organizing charities with those of London, Edinburgh, and Dublin. These studies became invaluable for Florence in her future plans in the field of nursing.

In 1854 Britain, France and Turkey declared war on Russia. English troops were sent to the Crimean Peninsula. Soldiers were dying at the front more from cholera and typhus than from gunshot wounds. To England's embarrassment, France was well prepared to tend the wounded, whereas the English had no means of caring for their casualties of war.

Sir Sydney Herbert, The English War Minister, was desperate to find someone to tend the soldiers under fire. He believed the most qualified to be Florence Nightingale. Because of her delicate health, Herbert hesitated to ask this of her. Finally, as the situation worsened in the Crimea, he wrote requesting help.

Few names in the ranks of outstanding women of history can produce the idyllic, noble, yet tender image that springs forth at the mention of the name Florence Nightingale...

Florence, fully aware of the problems in the Crimea, in turn was writing the War Minister, volunteering her services. The letters crossed in the mail. Herbert assured Miss Nightingale that, if she undertook this work, she would be given undisputed authority and complete support by the government.

She sailed to Scutari on the Black Sea with 38 nurses. Upon her arrival at the front she was confronted with work to which her genteel hands were not accustomed. At Scutari the army barracks had been turned into an emergency hospital with no furniture or medical supplies. It was filthy, damp and foul from the open sewers running beneath. Hundreds of wounded and sick men, many of them starving, frostbitten and half-naked, arrived from the battlefields.

One of Florence's first acts was to obtain brushes for cleaning. She set up a laundry in a nearby house, where bedding could be washed. She organized the kitchens. Many of the army doctors resented women interfering in their work, but that did not stop Florence.

It was here that the Nightingale legend was born. At night she would walk the long corridors, carrying her lantern, visiting the sick and wounded. She would speak to them and try to make them comfortable; very often she would sit with a soldier while he died. Florence looked like a saint to the wounded. History supports this by the following quote from a wounded soldier's letter home. "I kissed her shadow on my pillow."

> *Florence looked like a saint to the wounded. History supports this by the following quote from a wounded soldier's letter home. "I kissed her shadow on my pillow."*

She became a national heroine, adored by the English People. Florence may have been one of the first to be made famous by the media or the *paparazzi*, as we know it today. It was through a reporter, William Russell of the London Times, that her fame grew. It was he who gave her the name *The Lady with the Lamp*. Donations poured into the Nightingale Fund.

The war in the Crimea ended in 1856, and Florence returned to England. Brass bands and welcoming committees awaited her, but she would have none of it. Traveling under the name of Smith, she slipped unnoticed into London, caught a train to Derbyshire and arrived home alone, unannounced, to her family's astonishment.

Though thin and exhausted, she immediately went to work. She never forgot her *children,* the British soldiers. "I am a bad mother to come home and leave you in your Crimean graves," she wrote. She would not forget the thousands of men who, before the arrival of Florence and her nurses, had died from preventable diseases, not from war wounds.

In 1857, through Florence's efforts, a Royal Commission was set up to examine the army medical service. So that the calamity not be repeated, she inspected barracks and army hospitals, drew up charts and compiled a 1,000-page document, stressing the importance of good hygiene and a balanced diet in preventing disease.

During the remaining half century of her life, Florence worked on countless projects to help the sick and poor. First, she turned her attention to the general state of hospitals in England that were woefully inadequate and unhealthy. She wrote a book about hospital design that was filled with tables, charts, diagrams and ways of improving hospital plans. She undertook a three-year study of the health of mothers and newborn children. The Nightingale Training School was set up in the newly built St. Thomas' Hospital in London. The trainees (called Nightingale Nurses) received a thorough medical education. "To be a good nurse," she wrote, "one must be a good woman." From her pioneering work grew the whole of our modern nursing profession.

Florence continued working until her late seventies. She still offered advice and wrote hundreds of letters. She even found time to write a huge volume setting out her thoughts on religion and philosophy. Florence had definite ideas on religion, with particular concern for those she felt could be destined for the Netherworld. Then, as her eyesight failed, she withdrew increasingly from the outside world.

In 1907 Florence, now very frail, was awarded the Order of Merit, an honor never before bestowed on a woman in England. Three years later she died peacefully in her sleep at the age of ninety.

Florence had always hated the idea of being a celebrity. At her own request she was buried in simple style at a village church near her family's New Forest home. The words on her memorial stone read simply "FN Born 1820. Died 1910."

At a military dinner, at the close of the Crimean war, each guest was asked to write on a slip of paper the person who would be longest remembered. When the papers were examined all agreed on one name—*Florence Nightingale*.

Look for These Traits in Florence's Handwriting

1. Thinking processes,
Logical: rounded *m*'s
and *n*'s and flat-topped *r*'s
Quick: needle-like
retracements of the *m*'s
and *n*'s
Analytical: v-shaped
wedges come down to
the baseline

2. Dignity: If *d-* and *t-*
stems are retraced, dignity
is implied. A higher degree
of worth, repute and honor
is implied.

3. Decisiveness: Firm
endings on final strokes.
The writer has little trouble
making up his or her mind.

4. Diplomacy: When
writing tapers in size toward
the end of a letter formation, especially in the letters
m and *n*, diplomacy is
apparent. This can also be
seen when letters in a word
taper. The writer will use
tact in dealing with people.

5. Responsibility,
desire for: Large initial
clockwise loops, particularly
on capital letter structures,
indicate a desire for responsibility. The writer is willing
to take on additional duties.

6. Emotional respon-
siveness: This is seen in
the far-forward slant of the
writing. In a far-forward
slant, the heart rules the
feelings (see dictionary).

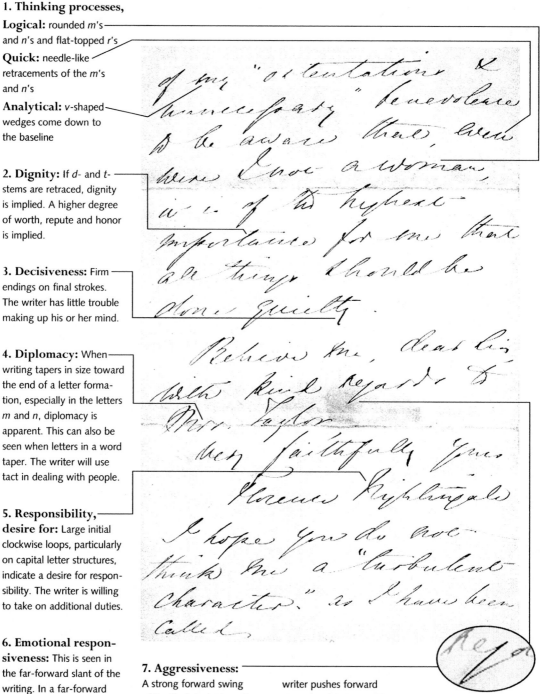

7. Aggressiveness:
A strong forward swing
of the final stroke in such
letters as the *g* and *y* can
show aggressiveness. The
writer pushes forward
strongly, resisting anything
or anyone that could
obstruct a planned course
of action.

What Handwriting Reveals About Florence

WE HAVE IN front of us the picture of a lady-like woman in a bonnet, raised in Victorian England. Surprisingly, the character traits of her handwriting that jump out at us indicate a woman who was far from the demure person we imagined. She had the spirit of aggressiveness that acts on opportunity. No grass grew under Florence's feet. We see this in the marked forcefulness of breakaway strokes of the *y* and *g*. Aggressiveness served as a catalyst in her personality, moving other traits into action.

> **No grass grew under Florence's feet. We see this in the marked forcefulness of breakaway strokes of the *y* and *g*.**

Florence had an active, emotional readiness, seen in the far-forward slant of her handwriting. When her heart was appealed to, she would respond. The initial loops in capital letters such as the *N* of Nightingale show that she could assume responsibility. She would do so willingly. Dignity, seen in the retraced *t*'s, shows that if a job was worth doing at all, it was worth doing well and to the best of her ability. This inner desire to be well-thought-of was a great motivator in her personality.

Quick thinking, seen in the needle-like retracements of the *m*'s and *n*'s, enabled Florence to grasp quickly the presence of a problem or the need for action. As a support of this ability, Florence had common sense. She thought things through in a methodical way and then acted. We see this in the rounded lower case letters. She would also analyze each piece of information before her, making her mind a formidable instrument that she used with agility. Wedges at the bottom of lower case letters show us this.

It was upon many of the above personal standards and attributes that she built *The Nightingale Nursing School*. We see other qualities in her personality that she manifested in her life and fostered in her school:

Dignity: She showed a high degree of worth, repute and humor (retraced *t*- and *d*-stems).

Diplomacy: She could be tactful with people (diminishing *m*'s and *n*'s).

Decisiveness: She had little trouble making up her mind (firm endings of final strokes).

Florence felt that for her students to become good nurses, they must set a high standard for themselves.

The Lady with the Lamp was not a myth, but a reality. Her handwriting shows us her courage and fortitude. Florence Nightingale, a slightly built young lady of 34, born to a life of ease and comfort, went down into the bloody fields of death in the Crimea where she brought mercy, light, hope and love to wounded and dying English soldiers.

CHAPTER 16

GEORGIA O'KEEFFE

1887–1986

"A man may lie, simulate, disown himself: A portrait may
change or beautify him: a book can lie and so can
a letter, but in one thing a man is inseparably
attached to the innermost truth of
his nature—his handwriting."

STEPHAN ZWEIG, AUSTRIAN AUTHOR, 1881–1942

GEORGIA O'KEEFFE was born on a large dairy farm near Sun Prairie, Wisconsin. Both her grandmothers—strong frontier women—passed along their creative spirit to Georgia. They dabbled in the art of painting. Grandmother O'Keeffe's paintings of fruit and moss rose were hung in the farmhouse.

When she was twelve, Georgia and her sisters began taking private drawing and painting lessons. Each Saturday they traveled seven miles, round-trip, by horse and buggy. The girls were taught to copy pictures from a stack of prints the teacher kept. It was in this class that Georgia discovered she liked to paint with watercolors. When she returned home, she would draw an imaginary scene of her own, such as palm trees waving in the ocean breeze. She hated it when her teacher touched up her paintings.

One day, that same year, Georgia confided in a friend that she wanted to be an artist. She didn't know why, because she had neither met a professional artist nor read about one. Her only inspiration was a small pen and ink drawing of a Grecian maiden in one of her mother's books. Georgia wanted to create something as beautiful as that drawing. The women in her family were educated; she too would go on with her education.

She studied at the Art Institute of Chicago and the Art Students League of New York. After several years of disappointments, as an artist, Georgia made a big decision. She would no longer try to please a teacher or attempt to copy a well-known artist. She would go beyond the rules and create charcoal images that were hers alone. Georgia suddenly realized how much she had to say, going through stacks upon stacks of sketch paper.

A friend showed these charcoal images to Alfred Stieglitz, the New York avant-garde photographer of The 291 Gallery, who expressed his joy in "the purest, finest, sincerest things that have entered my studio in a long while." Georgia, who had been teaching Art at West Texas State Normal College, returned to New York where, in 1924, she and Stieglitz were married.

During the long winter months in New York, she began to paint very large flowers, still some of her most popular works today. These precisely painted, heavily symbolic flowers became her signature work. They were exotic, oversized and filled the canvas with outrageous and heavy color, like close-up photographs, every detail perfectly painted. O'Keeffe took an object that, in reality, might be an inch in size and enlarged it to 48 inches.

> *"Most people in cities rush around so, they have no time to look at a flower. I want them to see it whether they want to or not."*

The largest was the six by seven-foot tall Miracle Flower. The viewer was stunned by the physical size of her paintings. This is what she gave to the world. Her bold patterns and clear coloring made her a pioneer in this style. As Georgia put it, "I found I could say things with color and shapes that I couldn't say in any other ways—things I had no words for."

When holding a flower in the cup of her hand and examining it closely, she said "It is my world for the moment; I want to give it to someone else. Most people in cities rush around so, they have no time to look at a flower. I want them to see it whether they want to or not." In 1938, James W. Lane wrote in Apollo Magazine, "The observer feels like Alice after she had imbibed the *Drink-me* phial." Another writer imagined her colossal flowers as a *boutonniere* for Gargantua.

In many of her paintings she used dark colors. *Pansy*, painted in 1925, and *Black and Purple Petunias* in 1926, are examples. She, too, almost always wore black. To add to this individualistic style, she rarely signed her art. She was a rebel at heart.

These giant flower paintings were first exhibited in 1925. In 1928 *A Cala Lily* would sell for $25,000, proving that Georgia could make a living with the strokes of her paintbrush.

Stieglitz disliked change of any kind, but Georgia had a great need to travel, to explore new places, to satisfy her artistic yearnings. She needed to see new landscapes and colors. Upon arriving in Taos, New Mexico, she knew it was hers. Georgia fell in love with every aspect of the land. She affectionately referred to northern New Mexico as *the faraway,* a place of stark beauty and infinite space.

She bought a *Model T Ford* and, being a loner, explored the land on her own. She removed the back seat, unbolted the front seat, turned it around and propped her canvas against the back wall of the car. It was here that she began a completely new style of painting. It was in this New Mexico wilderness that her stylized forms and motifs, such as cattle skulls, desert blooms and remote church crosses, began to dominate her work.

She returned to New York, but when springtime came, Georgia and Stieglitz were torn about whether she should spend yet another summer in New Mexico. Georgia's determination to return always overcame Stieglitz's wishes for her to remain in New York.

While in New Mexico, in 1934, she visited a ranch situated approximately 120 miles from Albuquerque. Georgia knew immediately that this was where she must live. In 1940 Ghost Ranch became hers, along with the view of the flat-topped mesa called Pedernal. She jokingly remarked, "It's my private mountain, it belongs to me. God told me if I painted it enough, I could have it." Among the guests who visited her were: D.H. Lawrence, Charles and Anne Lindbergh and Ansel Adams. "All the earth's colors of the painter's palette are out there in the miles of badlands," she would explain to her guests.

In December of 1945 Georgia expanded her holdings in New Mexico by purchasing an abandoned hacienda in the village of Aliguiu, sixteen miles from Ghost Ranch. She made extensive renovations to the five crumbling structures, until the original hacienda was resurrected. She was becoming an established New Mexican.

Stieglitz suffered a cerebral thrombosis in 1946. Georgia was able to be with him when he died. He had been her husband and companion, as well as her business manager and greatest critic. It was he who directed the distribution and sale of her works, which contributed greatly to her success. His photographs were important to Georgia. Many of them were private pictures of her. She spent the next three winters in New York, cataloging his work.

After Stieglitz's death Georgia began to travel extensively, but New Mexico would always be her home. Her paintings were shown in art institutes around the country. Her popularity skyrocketed, as did the value of her paintings.

Alfred Stieglitz's photographs were important to Georgia. Many of them were private pictures of her.

In 1971 her eyesight began to fail but she continued to paint watercolors, with assistance, until 1979. During the 1970s Juan Hamilton, a young potter and handy man, appeared at Georgia's door, looking for work. She would eventually hire him full-time. He became her closest confident, as well as her companion and business manager till her death. "He came just the moment I needed him." she told friends.

Georgia became increasingly frail and, in 1986, died at the age of ninety-eight. She instructed Juan Hamilton that, after her cremation, he was to climb to the top of Padernal, "the mountain God gave me," and scatter her ashes to the wind.

In 1997 the Georgia O'Keeffe Museum opened in Santa Fe, New Mexico, showing semi-abstractions based on nature, animal skulls and close-ups of flowers. New Mexico's desert is a principal inspiration, and O'Keeffe's depictions of dry hills and adobes are instantly recognizable.

Perhaps, the most extraordinary and singular gift Georgia O'Keeffe gave to her country was her native inspiration. Many artists felt that they were required to travel to Europe to study under the masters. Georgia relied on her intuitive intelligence and her ability to absorb and translate her surrounding environments onto the canvas. These combined to refine and polish her talents. As we look at her canvases and admire her work, we see that Georgia was American to the core.

There have been many explanations about the subtleties and connotations of her paintings. To this Georgia would say, in her outspoken manner, that the observer could interpret her paintings as he or she wished; suffice it to say that her paintings exemplified who Georgia O'Keeffe was.

During her legendary life of ninety-eight years, she made over two hundred flower paintings and countless other colorful interpretations of New York and New Mexico. She received many awards, including the highest honor for an American citizen: The United States Medal of Freedom.

Look for These Traits in Georgia's Handwriting

1. Broad-Mindedness:
Well-rounded, circle letters
a, e, d, g, q and *o* imply
broadmindedness, openness
to new ideas.

2. Defiance: The buckle
of the *k* should be in the
lower case area. If it rises
above this area in the writing, this is an indication of
defiance. The writer shows
resistance to authority or
opposition.

3. Imagination:
Occurrence of loops in the
writing points to imagination. The more inflated the
loops, the greater the imagination (see dictionary).

4. Fluidity: Smooth,
flowing strokes connecting
words often seen as a
figure-8, indicate ease
of expression. The writer
expresses him or herself
easily in writing,
speaking or acting.

5. Deliberateness:
Separated stems, slightly
rounded at the top, imply
that the writer is deliberate,
prone to move slowly in
carrying out a task.

6. Emotional Depth:
Seen in the heaviness of the
writing. Heaviness of the
writing indicates the deeply
felt emotions of the writer.

*Georgia's writing is a letter
written to Nadya Olyanova
in the 1950s.*

**7. Emotional
Response:** The slant of
the writing determines the
type of emotional response
of the writer. In the case of
Georgia's writing, the slant
is variable, but predomi-
nantly vertical and to the
left (see dictionary).

8. Decisiveness: Firm
final strokes in writing indicate decisiveness. The writer
has little difficulty making
up his or her mind.

9. Showmanship:
Oversized, ornate writing
especially in capitals,
displays the desire to be
noticed. When done with
taste and simplicity,
showmanship is indicated.

10. Cultural Desires:
A Greek *e* formation
indicates a desire for
culture. The writer desires
refinement of thought,
emotions, manners and
taste.

What Handwriting Reveals about Georgia

THE SPECIMEN OF handwriting appears to have been painted rather than written, so great is the heaviness of the strokes on the paper. Georgia could soak up emotions like a blotter; her senses could become filled with color and then overflow onto the canvas. She felt emotional experiences deeply; they could have a lasting impression on her. The heavy, yet clean lines of her writing indicate that she enjoyed pleasures, stimulated by vibrant colors, materials and tones. Forms, feeling and fragrances of life were important to her. This strong trait in her personality could be a dominating force in her life, affecting everything she did. Georgia exemplified this best when she said, "One cannot paint New York as it is, but rather as it feels."

The heavy, yet clean lines of her writing indicate that she enjoyed pleasures stimulated by vibrant colors, materials and tones.

As we look further at her handwriting, certain creative qualities become apparent. Ease of expression filled her writing, shown by the way in which words and letters flow easily from one to another and by the figure-eight formation, seen in the letters *sh* of *should*. Georgia's vivid imagination is seen in the inflated loops of her writing. This could enable her to reach out to that which was tasteful and refined, made evident by Greek *e*'s. Complementing this creativity is the slant of her script, which was variable; she went where her feelings and insights took her. She would not be confined to one way of looking at things. Added to this creativity was the fact that she could be receptive to new ideas, seen in the broad *e* in the word *written*. It should be noted that reserve is shown in the left direction and vertical angles of Georgia's writing. She found it difficult to get close to people and to have anyone too close to her; she would remain aloof.

The trait of deliberateness is seen on the third line, in the formation of the letter *t* in *went*, showing that she could take her time coming to a decision. However, once her mind was set, she could deal decisively and effectively with a situation or task. The strong endings of strokes indicate this.

Georgia had a rebellious attitude toward authority that she could defy with vigor, seen in the defiant *k*. She did what she wanted to do regardless of what anyone thought. She rejected rules and regulations and lived by her standards. However, showmanship, seen in the flair and flow of capital letters and all of her writing, could usually overcome any difficulties of this nature.

Georgia's character jumps out from the page as we look at her handwriting. She was no shrinking violet. Her paintings seem to speak clearly and appealingly to the Twenty-first Century, bringing a glimpse of the beauty of nature into our highly technological times.

> **Georgia had a rebellious attitude toward authority that she could defy with vigor, seen in the defiant *k*.**

CHAPTER 17

ANNA PAVLOVA

1881–1931

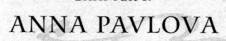

Dark words on white paper bare the soul.

GUY DE MAUPASSANT, FRENCH AUTHOR, 1850–1893

D ID ANNA PAVLOVA'S mother suspect, when she took her young daughter to a performance of *The Sleeping Beauty* at the Maryinsky Theatre, home of the Russian Kirov Ballet, how long a shadow the event would cast? Swept up by the magic of the performance, young Anna resolved, while dancers floated dreamlike before her, that one day she would be the beautiful Princess Aurora.

After years of training, Anna was finally accepted into the Imperial School of the Maryinsky Ballet. With her weak feet, poor turnout, a scrawny body and bad placement, a ballet career seemed doubtful. Added to these discouraging facts, she seemed shy, unsociable and introverted; friendships were few.

When she graduated from Maryinsky, the dancers of that era were strong, muscular ballerinas who had mastered multiple jumps and other technical *tricks*. Anna lacked the strength for such demands; her delicate, highly arched feet were too weak for the flamboyant *Pointe* work coming into style.

> *With her weak feet, poor turnout, a scrawny body and bad placement, a ballet career seemed doubtful.*

Ultimately, Anna made a virtue of her over-arched feet. She cleverly devised a supportive, leather shank and platform, inserted into soft *Pointe* shoes to support the metatarsal of the foot. She then pounded the platform to make it bigger and flatter and darned it to hold its shape. This modification conserved her energy and let her balance in *arabesque* style in ways that left audiences breathless. This had never been done before, but no ballerina, today, attempts toe-work without its equivalent.

Anna made the most of what she had: extension, a pliable torso, feminine delicacy and tremendous expressiveness. Add to this her diligent study with great masters of the dance, and one senses the significance of her gift.

The young girl who was once part of the audience for *The Sleeping Beauty* at the Maryinsky Theatre, soon excelled in such ballets as: *Giselle, Don Quixote* and *Les Sylphides.* Her exquisite, Romantic style, was showcased in these dances.

She is best remembered in *The Dying Swan.* As the title suggests, the ballet evokes the last moments in the life of a swan. A lone dancer moves softly in a single spotlight, torso bending expressively, arms extended in weightless motion. Her soft, bird-like curved arms, flutter until she gracefully expires, seated with her body bent over one, outstretched leg.

The Dying Swan is a simple dance, but few, if any, have captured the elusive magic of this ballet, as did Pavlova. Unfortunately, *The Dying Swan* has been an easy target for satire, even melodrama, but when done well it is powerful and exquisitely moving, as Pavlova's performances proved.

She continued to dance in her home theater until 1913, when she left Russia, never to return. England became her home. She toured with her company through the Americas. Her appearances in cities, villages and towns across the United States brought glimpses of fairyland to hundreds of thousands who had never seen ballet before, and many who would probably never see it again. She was a tireless traveler, bringing ballet into the lives of millions in Egypt, Burma, South Africa, Malay, Costa Rica, Australia, Java and many other countries.

The miracle of Pavlova was not the dance, but how she performed it. She was criticized for her taste and, at times, for her artistic judgment, but never for her ability to touch her audience. Anna sent forth a radiance that touched everyone, passing on the magic she had felt as a child. She was the *Prima Ballerina.*

Anna Pavlova was indisputably one of ballet's greatest ambassadors and the most influential ballerina of the Twentieth Century. In 1931, at age 50, Pavlova contracted a severe case of pleurisy. She chose not to have an operation that would leave her unable to dance. The pleurisy worsened and finally took her life. As she lay dying, she is reported to have opened her eyes, raised her hand and uttered these last words. "Get my swan costume ready."

A few days later, at show time in the theatre where she was to have performed *The Dying Swan,* the houselights dimmed, the curtain rose and, while the orchestra played Saint-Saen's familiar score, a spotlight moved around the empty stage, as if searching in the places where Pavlova would have been.

In her own words: "What exactly is success? For me it is to be found, not in applause, but in the satisfaction of feeling that one is realizing one's ideal. When a small child...I thought that success spelled happiness. I was wrong. Happiness is like a butterfly which appears and delights us for a brief moment, but soon flits away."

...the curtain rose, and while the orchestra played...a spotlight moved around the empty stage, as if searching in the places where Pavlova would have been.

Look for These Traits in Pavlova's Signature

1. Acquisition: An initial hook indicates acquisition or the desire to obtain or possess. Large hooks indicate a desire for important possessions. Small hooks imply that the writer craves trivial things.

2. Will Power: A relatively heavy *t*-bar (in this case it is the bar above Pavlova's signature) is evidence of a strong will. When the cross-bar is long, enthusiasm is added.

3. Self-Control: When said cross-bar is bent in a dome-like bow, it implies bending of the will. In Pavlova's case the bent stroke is above her signature. This trait suggests that the writer is trying to overcome a habit.

Pavlova's signature was the only handwriting available to us. Her signature comes from Klara Roman's book: Handwriting a Key to Personality *(1952).*

4. Emotional Depth: Pressure of the writing instrument or heaviness of the writing indicates how deeply an emotional situation will affect the writer.

5. Emotional Response: The slant of the writing determines emotional response. Far-forward slant indicates that the heart rules the writer's feelings (see dictionary).

What Her Signature Reveals About Pavlova

THE DISCIPLINE THAT is necessary in the life of a ballet dancer is evident in the sweeping, bowed line above Pavlova's signature. It becomes a canopy, nearly covering her whole name. The bend of this stroke indicates the ability to control her strong will. The length of the stroke shows enthusiasm, revealing her zeal and fervor in the pursuit of her interests. Her will to succeed was a dominating force in her life. It should be noted that will power, self-control and enthusiasm are all seen in the same heavy cross-bar above Pavlova's signature.

will power, self-control and enthusiasm are all seen in the same heavy cross-bar above Pavlova's signature.

The beginning hook in the *A* of *Anna* shows desire to acquire. In Pavlova's case this was not a desire for material acquisitions, but rather a desire for accomplishment in her art form. The hesitation and concentration, at the beginning of the stroke, show a buildup of ink, indicating great depth of feeling, which intensifies this desire to acquire.

The far-forward slant of her handwriting shows that her emotions were easily stirred; the heaviness of the strokes indicates that emotional experiences were deeply felt. This explains why audiences were captivated; her pen mirrored the underlying emotions the ballets portrayed. It mattered not what she danced, but how she danced that made her the idol of millions.

Pavlova was not known for her multiple *pirouettes*, but rather for her dancing, which became an airy, effortless spirituality, pervading her very being. The slant and depth of her signature show perfection in the communication of that radiance, which is the heart of ballet.

These few strokes of Pavlova's signature tell us a great deal about this remarkable *Prima Ballerina* who found success not in applause, but in the realization of an ideal.

CHAPTER 18

EVITA PERON

1919–1952

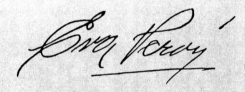

Critics, who flatly say there is nothing in handwriting analysis, are simply wrong.

GORDON ALLPORT. PROFESSOR OF PSYCHOLOGY,

HARVARD UNIVERSITY, 1946

"YES, I CONFESS that I have one single, personal ambition. I would like the name Evita to figure somewhere in the history of my country." This quote from her autobiography suggests the passion Evita possessed, a passion to help the working classes. Fifty years after her death, Argentina's heroine continues to live on in the hearts of her people who hope for better days.

Eva Duarte was born in 1919 in a small Argentine village. At the age of 15, to escape poverty, she moved to Buenos Aires in pursuit of an acting career. The city of Buenos Aires exerted a powerful magnetic attraction for rural Argentina. Her career as an actress began by playing minor roles in small theaters. She progressed slowly, building a reputation in radio and film.

Fifty years after her death, Argentina's heroine continues to live on in the hearts of her people, who hope for better days.

She became known as Evita and, as a young actress, struggled to make ends meet, always finding time to give a helping hand to others. At age 25 she met Juan Peron, while attending a fund-raiser held for victims of the 1944 San Juan earthquake. The following year she came to Juan's rescue, when he was imprisoned for his activity as an advocate for the working classes. One source told us that, through her reputation as an actress and her influence on radio, she helped to mobilize his followers, greatly contributing to Peron's release from prison on October 17, 1945. Other sources claim that it was not Evita, but Peron's followers who converged on the Government House and caused his release. As with many of the incidents surrounding Evita, it is difficult to sort fact from fiction. One thing we know, for a fact, is that she and Juan were married five days later.

Juan Peron became president of Argentina in 1946, and Evita quickly became the most relevant woman in Argentinean history. Strikingly beautiful, she could have anything she desired. She had a fascination for beautiful clothes from such fashion houses as Dior, in France, and expensive jewelry that was often gifted to her. When first coming to power, she maintained the image of a movie star, dressing elegantly. But, as Evita became involved in the cause of the *descamisados* (the shirtless workers), she underwent a transformation, slowly shedding her rich lifestyle. She formed the Evita Peron Foundation, which directed welfare and charity programs. These programs made her loved by the working class.

The opera and movie, *Evita,* have given people throughout the world a mistaken idea of who Evita truly was. In fact, Evita and Juan lived a simple life in the Residence. They were too engrossed in their country's problems to entertain lavishly. However, on official occasions and, as the wife of the president, Evita always maintained a glamorous and stylish image, dressing impeccably.

One of the climactic events in the life of Evita was her post-World War II tour of Europe, when she was presented to Franco in Spain and Pope Pius XII in Rome. As great as these moments were in the life of this poor girl from the Pampas of Argentina, she felt that one of her greatest life achievements was obtaining the vote for women in Argentina.

In Evita's seven years, as the first lady of Argentina, she commanded a vast and faithful political following. She had been the bridge between Peron and the people and was literally adored by the masses. When she died of cancer, at the early age of 33, that bridge collapsed. On her deathbed she begged Juan that she not be forgotten. He fell from power, before the impressive mausoleum he planned for her could be built. With her youth, glamour, adulation, agony and premature death, Evita's tragic fate fed the Argentinean working class with sentimentality like nothing else in the country's history.

In 1987 a small Argentina publishing house published a document found in the government archives in Buenos Aires. The document was referred to as: *Mi mensaje* or *My Message* and appeared to be the long-lost deathbed manuscript of Evita Peron.

The text of *My Message* has to be read in the context of the facts as we know them, as well as in the legends that have blossomed around Evita. The document illuminates her as both real and legendary. All things considered, she left an indelible, yet controversial mark on Argentina. At her death she was considered the most powerful woman in the world.

In 1955, when Juan Peron was overthrown in a military coup, the works of the Evita Peron Foundation were systematically destroyed. Adela Caprile, one of those designated to intervene in the dismantling of the Foundation said, "Evita cannot be accused of having kept one peso in her pocket..." Even after her death, the military so feared her influence that they destroyed nearly everything Evita stood for. This included an attack on her coffin. These horrific actions became believable, when it was revealed that those who governed the country tortured and killed 30,000 of their own citizens during the Dirty Wars of the 1970s and 1980s. Evita's body now lies in a tomb in the Recoleta cemetery in Buenos Aires, where admirers and tourists keep a constant vigil.

> *This quote of Evita's is a tribute to this remarkable woman: "I would willingly die a thousand deaths for my descamisados."*

Evita, in life, with her arms outstretched, gave her people an embrace of justice and love, which was her way of reducing the gap between social classes. Although Evita's Foundation did not survive, it incorporated a permanent list of problems, some solved, some half-solved, and many not solved at all. These problems became permanent issues, to be tackled by successive Argentinean governments. Evita left the people a bigger than life image, which remains even today.

This quote of Evita's is a tribute to this remarkable woman: "I would willingly die a thousand deaths for my *descamisados.*" This could fittingly be her epitaph. It came from her heart, as did everything she said or did.

Look for These Traits in Evita's Signature

Evita's signature was the only handwriting available to us. It came from the title page of La Razon de mi Vida, and has been considerably enlarged.

1. Thinking, keen comprehension:
Needle-like retracing indicates an instant grasp of subjects with which the writer is familiar. It is seen in the *r* of Peron.

2. Self-Confidence:
Good sized capital letters, indicate a good to strong self-esteem.

3. Thinking, analytical: When *v*-shaped wedges came down to the baseline, the writer shows analytical ability, the deeper the wedges, the more penetrating the analytical ability.

4. Cultural Desires:
A desire for culture may be present if there are Greek letter *e*'s in the writing. The writer shows refinement of thought, emotions, manners and taste. In Evita's case, the Greek *e* is found in the letter *r*.

5. Determination:
Heavy down strokes below the base line gives evidence of determination. The writer shows an indication of being resolute or having firmness of purpose.

6. Self-Reliance:
Underscored names indicate self-reliance. The writer wants to accomplish his or her aims without help from others.

7. Talkative:
Open-topped letter formations, especially in the *a* and *o*, indicate talkativeness; a desire to communicate (see dictionary).

What Her Signature Reveals About Evita

EVITA'S LIFE WAS shrouded in myth and legend. This made it difficult to know the real woman. Let us see what Evita's signature reveals as she moves her pen across the paper to sign her name.

She came from a simple background and lacked training in the style of the socially elite. However, Evita showed an inner desire for culture and refinement, seen in the *r* of Peron, which becomes a Greek *e*.

Evita had a burning desire to help her people. However, this desire ran much deeper. This was the driving force in her life and is seen in the powerful determination stroke of the *n* in Peron. The downstroke of an *n* usually stops at the baseline, but, in Evita's case,

This was the driving force in her life and is seen in the powerful determination stroke of the *n* in Peron.

it continues strongly, telling us that no matter what the obstacle might be, she would continue on. She was doggedly determined to help the struggling underprivileged, for she had been one of them.

Her ability to communicate to the masses of Argentina becomes obvious, when we look at her signature. She loved to speak, shown in the openness of the circle letters such as the *o* in Peron. She knew what she wanted to say, because she could form fast mental pictures, revealed in the points at the top of the letters. Once having the facts, she could quickly sift through them, selecting only the essential data, seen in the analytical points of her script. Add to this the far-forward slant of her writing, and we have a woman who was not only passionate about her causes, but could communicate that passion.

Her self-reliance, indicated in the underscore of her signature, and self-confidence, revealed in the large capitals, *E* and *P*, sustained her in her efforts to lift the masses out of poverty. Rejected by the elite, she turned to her own, the ones who understood her and whom she understood; the working masses, living in poverty.

Evita Peron represented solidarity, dignity and love for her country. She figured definitively in the history of Argentina. Her signature parallels her life.

CHAPTER 19

ELEANOR ROOSEVELT

1884–1962

Look then into thine heart and write.

Voices of the Night, HENRY WADSWORTH LONGFELLOW,

AMERICAN POET, 1807–1882

"YOU GAIN STRENGTH, courage, and confidence by every experience in which you really stop to look fear in the face. You must do the thing you think you cannot do." From *Eleanor and Franklin,* the story of their life together, based on Eleanor Roosevelt's private papers.

Eleanor had an anguished childhood. She was orphaned at age ten and raised by her grandmother in the tradition that dictated that children were to be seen and not heard. She retreated into herself.

She wrote, "I knew a child once who adored her father. She was an ugly little thing, keenly conscious of her deficiencies. Her father, the only person who really cared for her, would tell her how much he dreamed of her growing up...she must be truthful, loyal, and brave." This is an excerpt that came from *Eleanor and Franklin;* it tells the story of Eleanor's childhood. It speaks to us of how her life must have been. This lonely childhood would one day contribute to her profound sense of kinship with all of the desolate, deprived and excluded people of the world.

Eleanor attended her first dance at age 14. Her grandmother knew nothing of the fashionable styles for young ladies of that day. While other girls wore stylish, floor-length gowns, Eleanor's dress reached just to her knees. This fashion *faux pas* left long-legged Eleanor—who was taller than any of the other girls—feeling painfully wretched and self-conscious. While she stood on the sidelines trying not to burst into tears, a wonderful thing happened. Her handsome young cousin, Franklin Delano Roosevelt, whom she barely knew, came over and asked her to dance. Never had she been so grateful.

Eleanor went abroad to spend four years at Allenswood, a girls' finishing school outside London. The headmistress, Mademoiselle Souvestre, blessed with rare intuition, detected unusual qualities of mind and spirit in this awkward, badly-dressed American girl, whom she promptly took under her wing. Eleanor was one of few with whom the headmistress discussed world affairs. She spoke to her of the injustices of big nations toward smaller ones and the injustices of society to individuals; these were lessons that Eleanor learned well. Mlle. Souvestre also encouraged her to visit museums and other historic places, by herself, something that was unheard of at that time. She even suggested that Eleanor abandon the dresses her grandmother sent her and use her modest allowance to begin a stylish wardrobe.

Eleanor returned home, a poised young woman, with a Gibson-Girl figure and pleasant ways. Franklin took a second look, and a courtship began, which culminated in marriage in 1905. After a three-month honeymoon in Europe, they settled in New York. Eventually Franklin entered politics, becoming Governor of New York. In 1913 he was appointed assistant-secretary of the Navy. The last of their five children, Franklin Delano Jr., was born in 1914.

In the summer of 1921 Eleanor's mission in life was launched when Franklin was struck down by crippling polio.

In 1918 Eleanor received a crushing blow, while unpacking Franklin's luggage. She came upon information verifying her suspicions that he was having an affair with Lucy Mercer, a pretty young secretary Eleanor had hired. After months of a strained relationship, Eleanor and Franklin resolved to stay together. Lucy Mercer married shortly, thereafter.

This quote from Eleanor's book, *This I Remember,* exhibits her gracious spirit in the face of personal trauma, "Franklin might have been happier with a wife who was completely uncritical. That, I was never able to be; he had to find it in other people."

In the summer of 1921 Eleanor's mission in life was launched when Franklin was struck down by crippling polio. It was she who rose to the occasion by encouraging him to persevere, which made it possible for him to become president of the United States.

She worked in tandem with FDR to pull the country out of the depression. Eleanor practiced what she preached, regarding the necessity to *tighten the belt.* We were told of this incident by Cay Taylor, a graduate of Vassar

College: "The First Lady of the Land was asked to speak at Vassar. Her mode of transportation was by train, in coach style. The student body was amazed. It was a fine example of her earnestness about the plight of the country and the need to be frugal. She practiced what she preached."

Eleanor was able to go where the wheelchair-bound President could not. She was always there for him. We were not surprised to learn that her husband incorporated many of her ideas into the New Deal Social Welfare Program, as well as in a number of his other projects.

In the 1930s Eleanor received a request for an interview from a celebrated woman newswriter: Lorena Hickok. This was to blossom into a strong relationship. Hickok was a frequent dinner guest at the White house. There was a mutual respect for each other's achievements. Eleanor's life was one of fighting for causes and believing in people.

She hosted morale-boosting parties for army troops and braved the depths of coal mines to call attention to the conditions of the miners. It is quite possible that reaching out to others helped her to overcome her feelings of inadequacy and to satisfy lifelong yearning to be needed and loved.

After the death of Franklin, Eleanor went on to teach at a school she had founded for poor children. She ran a factory for jobless men and was an advocate for equal rights, when that was an unpopular thing to do. She put all her talents to use. No doubt her father's words continued to ring in her ears: I must be truthful, loyal and brave. Her career of championing the under-privileged culminated in her appointment by President Truman, as a delegate to the United Nations, where she helped to found UNICEF and assisted in the passage of the Universal Declaration of Human Rights.

As a delegate to the United Nations, Eleanor took an opposing position to Andrei Vyshinsky, regarding the return of East Europeans who had left their homeland during World War II. She argued that all human beings must have the right to choose. They should not be forced to live in a country where they would no longer be able to choose for themselves. Although she won, she made it a point to remain friendly with Vyshinsky who later invited her to visit the Soviet Union.

It was amidst these limitless roadblocks and difficult moments that Eleanor emerged victorious. It was she who, with great wisdom said, "No one can make you feel inferior without your consent." She never for a moment abandoned the virtues her father had instilled in her at an early age and to which she had dedicated herself.

The First Lady received countless awards, recognitions and accolades. She was made an honorary member of Phi Beta Kappa and received 34 honorary degrees from universities at home and abroad, including Smith College, the University of Utrecht, in the Netherlands, and Oxford.

Flags flew at half-mast everywhere, the first time this honor had been given the widow of a President.

On September 26, 1962, at the age of 78, this gallant woman entered the Columbia Presbyterian Medical Center for a routine checkup. She had been so long a tower of strength; no one could believe it was serious. The end came on November 7, 1962. Flags flew at half-mast everywhere, the first time this honor had been given the widow of a President. Three American Presidents, Eisenhower, Truman and Kennedy, attended the ceremony, where she was laid to rest in the Hyde Park Rose Garden, next to her husband. Representatives of 110 countries of the United Nations came, and glowing and eloquent tributes poured in from great personages the world over.

Look for These Traits in Eleanor's Handwriting

Eleanor's handwriting comes from, Eleanor and Franklin:
The Story of their Relationship, *based on Eleanor's Private Papers.*

1. Argumentative:
If the first upstroke of the letter *p* rises above the tops of the lower case letters, the writer shows argumentativeness.

2. Initiative: When an upstroke above the base line leaps forward sharply, such as in the letter *h*, the writer shows initiative. The writer has the ability to spot opportunities.

3. Defiance: The buckle of the letter *k* should be in the lower case area. When it rises above this area, defiance is indicated. The writer has a disposition to resist authority.

4. Thinking, quick: Retraced, needle-like, upward strokes, usually found in *m*'s and *n*'s. The writer thinks quickly, seeming to reach conclusions almost instantly.

5. Fluidity: Smooth -flowing strokes connecting words or letters, implies ease of expression.

6. Emotional Response: Slant determines emotional responsiveness or how quickly a writer responds to outside stimuli. Eleanor had a moderate to far-forward slant..

7. Diplomacy: When writing tapers, in size in a letter formation, especially in the letter *m* or *n*, or when letters in a word taper, diplomacy is apparent. The writer can use tact in dealing with people.

8. Decisiveness: When a firm final stroke is seen in writing, the writer has little difficulty making up his or her mind.

9. Determination: Heavy, long downstrokes below the base line give evidence of determination. This is an indication of having firmness of purpose and being resolute.

What Handwriting Reveals About Eleanor

ELEANOR WAS A warm and demonstrative person. She needed to reach out to people, and it was natural for her to do so. This is seen in the moderate to far-forward slant of her handwriting

She would always be ready to take the first step. She did not look over her shoulder to see if someone was there to help; she would plunge in and accomplish the task at hand. This shows itself in the initiative stroke of her *h*'s. She leaned on no one. The long downstrokes of her writing indicate an ability to follow through with determination. Added to this was decisiveness, seen in the firm ending of the strokes of her writing.

The flowing lines of Eleanor's handwriting that join one word to another were predominant in her writing and gave her great continuity of thought and ease of expression.

The flowing lines of Eleanor's handwriting that join one word to another were predominant in her writing and gave her great continuity of thought and ease of expression. Moreover, her ability to quickly assimilate information, seen in the needle-like retracing of the lower case *m*'s and *n*'s, enabled her to take effective action within moments. This called for flexibility on Eleanor's part and emotional maturity. One can see how comfortable she would be talking to coal miners, slum children or foreign delegates, given the qualities of character seen in the above traits of her handwriting.

Perhaps the handwriting traits that made Eleanor most effective, strange as it may seem, were defiance and argumentativeness. She had the ability to get what she wanted; she would not be pushed or forced by anyone against her will. This is shown in the defiant *k* of her writing. Strengthening this was her ease in putting up a stiff argument on matters of principle and opinion, indicated by the points of the *p*'s in her writing. She defended the children with UNICEF and confronted the stalwart and respected Daughters of the American Revolution when they denied Marian Anderson the right to sing at Constitution Hall because of her color. At the United Nations she stood up to ambassador Vischinsky when he would not give eastern Europeans the right to choose where they should live. Yes, Eleanor was defiant and argumentative, and she used these particular qualities to great advantage.

She was a warm, intelligent and diplomatic human being. These qualities are reflected in her handwriting. She was referred to as the First Lady of the World. A group of children from a public school in Brooklyn sent a *Remembrance Book* when she died. It contained this expression of love: "Eleanor Roosevelt was like a mother to the world, and we are like orphans because of her death." An orphan, herself, she never lost her touch with those less fortunate. Nor did she ever forget the words her father spoke to her as a child: she should be truthful, loyal and brave.

CHAPTER 20

QUEEN VICTORIA

1819–1901

Handwriting bears an analogy to the character

of the writer...

BENJAMIN DISRAELI, BRITISH STATESMAN. 1804–1881

V ICTORIA'S ENGLISH FATHER, the Duke of Kent, was the fourth son of George III. Her mother, the Duchess, was German. They were married in Germany, but it was essential that their child be born in England for her position in the succession to be strong. At Victoria's birth, she was fifth in succession to the throne. By the time she was eight months old, she was two degrees nearer the crown. She ascended the throne at the age of eighteen and became Queen of England and Ireland and, eventually, Empress of India, reigning for 64 years.

Victoria's upbringing was sheltered. As the only legitimate descendant of the vast family of George III, her life was precious and well-protected. She was a short, ordinary looking child. She wrote later, "We lived in a very simple and plain manner. Tea was allowed only as a great treat. I did not know what a happy domestic life was."

The Duke of Wellington said, "Had she been my own daughter, I could not have wished that she should do better. Why, she not only filled the chair, she filled the room!"

At 13 she was given a journal in which she recorded her daily activities. She kept a diary for the rest of her life. On June 20, 1837, she wrote, "I was awakened and told that the Archbishop of Canterbury wished to see me. He informed me that my uncle, the King, was no more...and that I am Queen."

At half-past eleven, that same day, Queen Victoria had her first Council. She bowed to the assembly, took her seat, and read her Declaration in a clear voice, without a hint of nervousness. "She went though the whole ceremony with perfect calmness and self-possession, but, at the same time, with a graceful modesty and propriety, interesting and ingratiating," wrote Greville, her diarist. The Duke of Wellington said, "Had she been my own daughter, I could not have wished that she should do better. Why, she not only filled the chair, she filled the room!"

The next morning bells tolled to commemorate the death of the king and then ceased to toll: "The King is Dead, Long Live the Queen!" was the cry of the people. The throne must never be empty.

After the Napoleonic Wars, the rest of Europe lay exhausted, but England, small though she was, remained uninvaded, undefeated. It was on that *tight little, right little island,* as the words of a contemporary song put it, that Victoria ascended the throne.

The young Queen threw herself into her new life with zest for both work and pleasure. Her diarist tells us that, "On Official duty, she was graceful, dignified and always under control, but, on unofficial occasions, the Queen was as natural as any girl of her age could have been...she laughs in real earnest, opening her mouth as wide as it can go...she eats quite as heartily as she laughs; I think I may say she gobbles...she blushes and laughs every instant, in so natural a way as to disarm anyone." This was a good illustration of who Victoria really was. She reacted the way she felt. Her public saw the other side of Victoria, a much more controlled queen.

Her marriage was on everyone's mind. She had many suitors, one, of whom, wore her picture in a locket around his neck and one around the neck of his dog. The Queen was not impressed.

There had been scheming since her birth that she and her cousin, Albert of Germany, would one day marry. The idea of such a union had been instilled in both children. Fortunately it was a meeting of hearts. Victoria was the one to propose, for, as Albert was of a lower rank, it was impossible for him to speak first. Her diary states that she asked him by saying, "Could you forsake your country for me? It would make me too happy if you would consent to what I wish."

After the marriage, life in England was not what Prince Albert had expected, having to bow to Victoria's every wish. Their difference in rank caused difficulties. Stories abound of how Albert handled this delicate situation. Once, after a quarrel, Albert retired to his study. The Queen tried the door and found it bolted.

"Who is there?" inquired the Prince in a calm voice.

"The Queen," came the haughty reply.

"The Queen must wait," answered the voice from within.

She was dumbfounded. Again and again, she beat upon the door and, again and again, came the answer, "The Queen must wait."

At last, in tears, the Queen sobbed, "Your wife, Albert, your poor, unhappy, Weibchen."

The door opened; Albert had made his point.

The first of Victoria's nine children was born in 1840. Albert watched over the Queen with devoted care. No one else ever lifted her from the bed to the sofa. "A kinder, wiser, or more judicious nurse could not be," wrote the Queen. Under the circumstances it seemed natural that he should read and discuss secret government dispatches and deal with her private dispatches. Gradually, he came into his own with growing authority.

The relationship between Victoria and Albert continued to improve with the arrival of each child. She set an example of respectability that millions admired and strove to emulate in their lives. Manners and civility were stressed. It was the beginning of the Victorian Age.

Albert watched over the Queen with devoted care. No one else ever lifted her from the bed to the sofa. "A kinder, wiser, or more judicious nurse could not be," wrote the Queen.

Meanwhile, Paris and Vienna were becoming the most elegant cities in Europe. Vienna was famous for music and dancing, Paris for fashion and art. Albert felt that England should not be overshadowed. In 1851, he was responsible for the *Crystal Palace Exhibition*, a highly profitable industrial convention, which was responsible for much of the popularity later enjoyed by the British Monarchy.

But there was a darker side to Victoria's England. Work was not equally well-rewarded. Many conditions were deplorable, especially in the slums of London. Novelist Charles Dickens in his novel, *Oliver*, made the plight of

English children very real. Jack the Ripper, the infamous murderer in the Whitehill Chapel section of London, added to this seamy side of London. Extravagant spending in Victoria and Albert's government occurred at the very time when the Irish potato famine was at its peak. England allowed the export of grain and cattle from Ireland to England, while over a million Irish peasants starved to death.

After Albert's death, at age forty-two, a desolate Queen remained in self-imposed seclusion for years.

Victoria went about her social life as though all was well, corresponding with friends, relatives and her own children. She wrote to an American friend, asking her to please find a sample of George Washington's writing to complete her collection of American Presidents' handwriting. She was an amateur water colorist, depicting daily life with tender pictures of her children. Victoria's home life and domesticity immediately bonded her with middle-class English families of that era; whatever Victoria and family did, they too, wanted to do.

When her mother passed away, Victoria was not just sad; she was overwhelmed with grief, weeping at the mention of her mother's name, almost wallowing in it. "This weeping...day after day...is my welcome friend," she wrote. Albert guided her through this difficult time.

After Albert's death, at age forty-two, a desolate Queen remained in self-imposed seclusion for years. Her genuine, but obsessive mourning, would occupy her for the rest of her life. She always wore black. Her black jewelry was known as *Jet*. There were shops in every English town selling Jet Jewelry; such was the influence of Victoria.

During her reign, Queen Victoria was the center of attention. Her influence governed the direction, ambition and ideals of her subjects. She was thrifty, but capable of giving; she was affectionate, even passionate, but rarely unbridled, at least publicly. As a mother she had definite ideas about the duties of children. She felt that God-given traits should never lie buried or unused.

All of these attributes began to mold the age, which was named for Victoria, a woman whose strong personality permeated the social structure of her realm and eventually, the world. What Victoria did, the world wanted to copy. Victoria's influence is still with us today: in architecture, interior decoration, clothing, and jewelry.

Victoria presided over the ascent to preeminent power of the world's first industrialized nation. She filled the thrones of Europe with her children and grandchildren, reined over the largest empire the world has ever seen and influenced society with her presence.

Look for These Traits in Victoria's Handwriting

Queen Victoria's handwriting is a letter written to Miss Mary Gordon, thanking her for the gift of a bible which had belonged to her brother, General C.G.Gordon. Windsor Castle, 16 March 1885.

1. Self-Control: A crossbar of the letter *t*, bent in a dome-like bow, indicates a bending of the will.

2. Diplomacy: When writing tapers in size toward the end of a letter formation, especially in the letters *m* or *n*, diplomacy is apparent. This can also be seen when a word tapers.

3. Caution: Caution is shown in words that end with a straight final stroke, usually at the end of a line. The cautious writer is reluctant to rush into situations or act rashly.

4. Jealousy: The jealousy stroke is a clockwise initial loop that is flattened or ovalled to at least some degree. It occurs at the beginning of a letter structure and it must be closed. The writer can show a fear of rivalry.

5. Will Power: A relatively heavy *t*-bar is evidence of strong will power. When the crossbar is long, enthusiasm is added; the longer the bar, the greater the enthusiasm.

6. Emotional Response: Is seen in the far-forward slant of the writing stroke. Slant determines how quickly the writer responds to outside stimuli.

7. Argumentative: If the first stroke of the letter *p* rises above the lower stroke, the writer shows argumentativeness. The writer will want to discuss or debate an issue.

8. Emotional Depth: Is seen in the heaviness of the writing line, which determines how deeply the writer feels.

9. Attention, desire for: The desire to attract attention is present if finals rise above the tops of a letter or word. When the finals turn back, the writer has an excessive desire to be noticed; he or she will constantly find ways to be noticed.

10. Determination: Heavy downstokes below the base line give evidence of determination; the width or heaviness indicates strength. The length indicates endurance.

11. Aggressiveness: A stroke that swings out boldly from the downstroke points to aggressiveness.

What Handwriting Reveals About Victoria

IN THE NINETEENTH Century Britannia ruled the waves, and Victoria ruled Britannia. The forcefulness of this woman is apparent in her handwriting. The single, most compelling strength in Victoria's personality was her ability to set strong goals in a purposeful and enthusiastic manner, seen in the high, sweeping *t*-crossings of her handwriting. She knew what she wanted, and she went for it. People recognized this and followed her lead. Having set her course, she could then follow through with enduring determination. This is seen in the long downstrokes below the baseline of her script. The aggressive strokes in her handwriting add to her powerful personality. Victoria would drive through an obstacle if she could not go around it.

The small, tight, initial clockwise loops, in the capital *M* and the small *h* of her handwriting, are examples of the envious side of Victoria; she was jealous of any rivalry.

The far-forward slant and the heaviness of her script reinforce the above impressions. Victoria's feelings were stored in her innermost being. She was not lukewarm; she was either hot or cold. The slant shows that she reacted immediately and strongly to outside stimuli; the heaviness indicates how deeply she felt. Note that the sample of her handwriting is on a page of her personal stationery, showing a heavy black border. Black became her signature color.

Victoria learned to control her strong emotions by developing caution, seen in the long, straight finals of words, especially at the end of a sentence. She also grew in the art of diplomacy, shown in the diminishing of words. Despite her caution and diplomacy, she would not back away from a discussion or debate and would defend her position with vigor, indicated in the height of the letter *p*. In matters of this nature, she would exercise self-control, which is seen in the dome-like bow of her *t*-crossings.

The small, tight, initial clockwise loops, in the capital *M* and the small *h* of her handwriting, are examples of the envious side of Victoria; she was jealous of any rivalry. It is said that Victoria's rivalry was so intense that she proclaimed herself Empress of India, when she found that her daughter had become Empress of Prussia. She wanted to be the center of attention, indicated by the reverse stroke of final letters.

Victoria's handwriting shows a woman with qualities needed in a leader: a good mind, strong will and determination. Complementing these attributes, she developed diplomacy, caution and self-control, qualities which came to her aid as Queen, especially in political situations. It was no accident that her influence governed the direction, ambition, and ideals of her subjects and cast an aura on the rest of the civilized world.

ACKNOWLEDGEMENTS

TO THOSE PROFESSIONALS, friends and family who have provided much needed guidance and support during the preparation of this book and to whom I shall be forever grateful: My husband Bill, for being my historian and editor; Our children, especially Ann who helped me through many difficult moments; Theresa Whitehill, Graphic Artist and Designer, for her talent and patience; Mildred Toledo for her invaluable assistance. I am also indebted to Khmasea Bristol, Hadley Hoover, Kathleen Allen-Meyer, and Yarrow Summers for their time and assistance.

Handwriting, Photograph, and Image Credits

Anderson

Photograph source, page 2. Portrait of Marian Anderson. 1935. Anderson Collection of Photographs, Annenberg Rare Book & Manuscript Library, Van Pelt-Dietrich Library Center, University of Pennsylvania, Philadelphia, PA.

Signature source, page 2. From portrait of Marian Anderson. 1955. Anderson Collection of Photographs, Annenberg Rare Book & Manuscript Library, Van Pelt-Dietrich Library Center, University of Pennsylvania, Philadelphia, PA.

Handwriting source, pages 2, 6. Note regarding Sibelius from a letter written in Helsinki, Finland, 1933. Marian Anderson Papers, Annenberg Rare Book & Manuscript Library, Van Pelt-Dietrich Library Center, University of Pennsylvania, Philadelphia, PA.

Handwriting, permission to use, pages 2, 6. DePreist, James. Maestro, Oregon Symphony and nephew of Marian Anderson. Special thanks to Mary Frances Byrne for her assistance.

Special thanks to Nancy M. Shawcross, Curator of Manuscripts, and John Pollack, Rare Book & Manuscript Library, University of Pennsylvania, for their assistance.

Joan of Arc

Oil painting source, page 9. *St. Joan Praises the Holy Spirit.* anonymous artist. Copyright © 1997, Frohlick, Virginia. Saint Joan of Arc Center, Albuquerque, New Mexico.

Signature source, pages 9, 14. Letter dictated and signed by Joan of Arc to the citizens of Riom, dated November 29, 1429. Medieval French. Joan of Arc Archive, France. Special thanks to Allen Williamson of the Joan of Arc Archives for his assistance.

Catherine II

Engraving source, page 17. Empress Catherine II Empress of Russia. Originally engraved for *The Eclectic* by Geo. E. Perine, NY, between 1850 and 1885. From *Europe From the Renaissance to Waterloo*, original publisher: D.C. Heath and Company. Licensed by ArtToday.com and ClipArt.com.

Handwriting source, pages 17, 20. Catherine's writing in archaic French, 1763. *Illustrated Supplement to The Psychology of Handwriting*, Saudek, Robert, Sacramento, CA: Books for Professionals, 1978.

Curie

Photograph source, page 24. Marie and Pierre Curie with bicycles. AIP Emilio Segrè Visual Archives, American Institute of Physics, College Park, Maryland. Special thanks to Heather Lindsay, Assistant Librarian and Photo Administrator, American Institute of Physics, for her assistance.

Handwriting source and permission to use, pages 24, 30. Marie Curie's writing in Polish to the American Red Cross, date unknown. *The Psychology of Handwriting*, Nadya Olyanova, Hollywood, CA: The Wilshire Publishing Company.

Didrickson Zaharias

Photograph source and permission to use, page 33. Babe Didrickson Zaharias, Wilson Sporting Goods promotional photograph. Babe Didrickson Zaharias Foundation, Inc., Beaumont, Texas.

Handwriting source, pages 33, 38. Letter to Petty Kirk Bell, date unknown. Bell, Peggy Kirk, Southern Pines, North Carolina.

Handwriting permission to use, pages 33, 38. Babe Didrickson Zaharias Foundation, Inc., Beaumont, Texas.

Special thanks to W.L. Pate, Jr., President, Babe Didrickson Zaharias Foundation, Inc., and Rhon Didrickson, nephew of Babe Didrickson Zaharias, for their assistance.

Duncan

Photograph source, page 40. Associated Press/Wide World Photos.

Handwriting source, pages 40, 46. Excerpt of a letter written to Victor Seroff in 1927. *The Real Isadora*, Victor Seroff, New York: The Dial Press, 1971.

Earhart

Photograph source, page 50. Atchison County Historical Society, Kansas. Special thanks to Chris Taylor for his assistance.

Photograph, permission to use, page 50. The Amelia Earhart Birthplace Museum, Kansas.

Handwriting, source and permission to reprint, pages 50, 58. A note from Amelia Earhart's log book written on her flight over the Atlantic in 1932. *Handwriting Tells*, Nadya Olyanova, Hollywood, California: Wilshire Book Publishing.

Keller

Photograph source and permission to use, page 62. Helen Keller and Alexander Graham Bell. Perkins School for the Blind, Research Library. Watertown, MA.

Handwriting source and permission to use, pages 62, 68. Excerpts of a letter written by Helen Keller at 11 years of age. Handwriting samples courtesy of Perkins School for the Blind, Watertown, MA.

Special thanks to Jan Seymour-Ford, Research Librarian, Kimberly Emrick Kittredge, Webmaster and Public Relations, and Terry Hiller, Publications, Perkins School for the Blind, for their assistance.

Lindbergh

Photograph source and permission to use, page 71. Anne Morrow Lindbergh. Photo by Richard W. Brown. The Charles A. and Anne Morrow Lindbergh Foundation, Anoka, Maine. Special thanks to Dacia Durham, the Charles A. and Anne Morrow Lindbergh Foundation, for her assistance.

Handwriting source and permission to use, pages 71, 76. Letter from Anne Morrow Lindbergh to her sister, Constance, 1930s. *Locked Rooms and Open Doors, Diaries and Letters of Anne Morrow Lindbergh, 1933–1935*, Anne Morrow Lindbergh, a Helen and Kurt Wolff Book, New York and London: Harcourt Brace Jovanovich, 1974.

Meir

Photograph source, page 80. Golda Meir Collection, 1904–1987, University Manuscript Collection 21, Archives, University of Wisconsin Libraries, Milwaukee, WI.

Handwriting source, pages 80, 86. Note written to Bernard Simpson in Vancouver, B.C., Canada by Golda, when she was in Ramat Avive, Israel, in 1977. Golda Meir Collection, 1904–1987. University Manuscript Collection 21, Archives, University of Wisconsin Libraries, Milwaukee, WI.

Special thanks to Charles Kempker and Jennifer Sullivan, Archives, Golda Meir Library, for their assistance.

Handwriting, permission to use, pages 80, 86. Meir, Menacham and Rahabi, Sara, son and daughter of Golda Meir. Tel Aviv, Israel. Special thanks to Anat Morahg, Tel Aviv, Israel, for her assistance.

Montessori

Photograph and Handwriting source and permission to use, pages 89, 94. The Association Montessori Internationale, Amsterdam, The Netherlands.

Montgomery

Photograph source, page 98. L.M. Montgomery Collection, Archival and Special Collections, McLaughlin Library, University of Guelph, Canada.

Handwriting source, pages 98, 104. A page from Lucy Maud Montgomery's diary, date unknown. L.M. Montgomery Collection, Archival and Special Collections, McLaughlin Library, University of Guelph, Canada.

Special thanks to Lorne Bruce and Darlene Wiltsie, University of Guelph, for their assistance.

Photograph and Handwriting, permission to use, pages 98, 104. Hebb, Marion, solicitor for the Lucy Maud Montgomery family estate.

Moses

Photograph source and permission to use, page 107. *Portrait of Grandma Moses at her painting table,* 1952. Ifor Thomas, Copyright © 1975 Galerie St. Etienne, New York, Grandma Moses Properties Co., New York.

Signature source, page 107. *Bunker on Evaluation*, M.N. Bunker and the IGAS Instruction Department, Chicago: International Graphoanalysis Society, 1970.

Handwriting source and permission to use, pages 107, 112. Excerpt from *Christmas,* Galerie St. Etienne, New York, Copyright © 1952 (renewed 1980), Grandma Moses Properties Co., New York. Special thanks to Jane Kallir and Kirsti Blom for their assistance.

Mother Teresa

Photograph source and permission to use on front cover. Pulice, Frank.

Photograph source, page 116. Mother Teresa, head of the Missionaries of Charity order, cradles an armless baby girl at her order's orphanage in Calcutta, India in 1978. Photo by Eddie Adams. Associated Press/Wide World Photos.

Handwriting source, pages 116, 120. Copy of Mother Teresa's original writing on a photo and prayer printed by the Knights of Columbus. Special thanks to Khmasea Bristol, New York, NY, for obtaining this copy, when in Cambodia in 1990.

Nightingale

Photograph source and permission to use, page 123. Miss Florence Nightingale. Courtesy of the Florence Nightingale Museum Trust, London. Special thanks to Jenny Möllergren, Administrator, and Sue Laurence, Curator, Florence Nightingale Museum Trust, for their assistance.

Signature source, page 123. *Collecting Autographs and Manuscripts*, Charles Hamilton, second edition, University of Oklahoma Press, 1961.

Handwriting source and permission to use, pages 123, 128. Clendenning History of Medicine Library, Medical Center, University of Kansas, Kansas City, KS. Special thanks to Dawn McInnis, Rare Book Library, Clendenning Library, for her assistance.

O'Keeffe

Photograph of Georgia O'Keeffe by Alfred Stieglitz (1864–1946) 1920/1922. Palladium print 4 1/2 x 3 9/16 inches. Gift of The Georgia O'Keeffe Foundation. Location: The Georgia O'Keeffe Museum, Santa Fe. Copyright © Georgia O'Keeffe Museum, Santa Fe / Art Resource, NY.

Permission to use handwriting. Lopez, Judy. The Georgia O'Keeffe Foundation. Abiquiu, New Mexico.

Special thanks to Ryan Jensen and Jennifer Belt, Art Resource, for their assistance.

Handwriting, permission to reprint, pages 132, 138. A letter from Georgia O'Keeffe to Nadya Olyanova in the 1950s. *The Psychology of Handwriting,* Olyanova, Nadya. Sacramento, California: Books for Professionals, 1971.

Pavlova

Photograph source and permission to use, page 142. Originally a post-card by Rotary Photo, E.C., Photography Collections, Special Collections Department, Albin O. Kuhn Library & Gallery, University of Maryland Baltimore County. Special thanks to John Beck, Assistant, Special Collections Department, Albin O. Kuhn Library, for his assistance.

Handwriting source and permission to reprint, pages 142, 146. *Handwriting a Key to Personality*. Roman, Klara G., New York: Pantheon Books, Inc., 1952.

Peron

Photograph source, page 148. Maria Eva Duarte de Peron waves to supporters in Buenos Aires, October 17, 1951. Associated Press/Wide World Photo, Archivo Clarin.

Handwriting source, pages 148, 152. Signature from title page of book, *La Razon de mi Vida*. Special thanks to Mariano Bayona Estraderu, Barcelona, Spain, for his assistance.

Roosevelt

Photograph source and permission to use, page 155. Eleanor Roosevelt. Courtesy of Franklin D. Roosevelt Presidential Library, Hyde Park, New York.

Handwriting source, pages 155, 160. *Eleanor and Franklin: The Story of Their Relationship*, Joseph P. Lash, New York: W.W. Norton and Company, 1971.

Handwriting, permission to use, pages 155, 160. Courtesy of Franklin D. Roosevelt Presidential Library, Hyde Park, New York.

Queen Victoria

Photograph source, page 164. Queen Victoria. From *Library of Universal History*, Volume 09, Original Publisher: Union Book Company. Licensed by ArtToday.com and ClipArt.com.

Handwriting source, pages 164, 170. Letter to Miss Mary Augusta Gordon, March 16, 1885. *Universal Classic Manuscripts*, Portfolio II, Manuscript Number 74, British Museum, Washington and London: T. Walter Dunne.

Handwriting, permission to use, pages 164, 170. Queen Victoria. 1885. MS. 34,483 ff. 7–8. The British Library. London, England. Special thanks to Zoe Stansell for her assistance.

BIBLIOGRAPHY

Anderson

Anderson, Marian. *My Lord, What a Morning*. New York: Macmillan, 1930.

Patterson, Charles. *Marian Anderson*. New York: Franklin Watts Inc. An Impact Biography, 1988.

Joan of Arc

Mabel Dodge Holmes. *Joan of Arc*. Philadelphia: The John C. Winston Company, 1930.

Shaw, Bernard. *Saint Joan*. Baltimore, Maryland: Penguin Books, 1924.

Stanley, Diane. *Joan of Arc*. New York: William Morrow and Company, Inc., 1988.

Zanoni, Michael M. *Printing, Writing and Document Related Chronology*. Mill Valley, California: Celebrity Access Publications, 1995.

Catherine II

Duncan, David Douglas. *The Kremlin*, New York: The Cross River Press Ltd., 1979.

Karohs, Erika. *Russian Alphabet, Encyclopedia for Handwriting Analysts*. Pebble Beach, California: Self-published, 1985.

Toyat, Henri. *Catherine the Great, A biography*. New York: Elsevier-Dutton Publishing Co. Inc., 1980.

Zwingle, Erla. *Catherine the Great*. Washington, D.C.: National Geographic Magazine, September, 1998.

Curie

Birch, Beverly. *Marie Curie*. Milwaukee: Gareth Stevens Publishing, 1988.

Conner, Ewina. *Great Lives: Marie Curie*. New York: The Bookwright Press, 1987.

Curie, Eve. *Madame Curie: A Biography by Eve Curie*. New York: Doubleday, 1938.

Karohs, Erika, *Polish Alphabet, Encyclopedia for Handwriting Analysts*. Pebble Beach, California: self-published, 1985.

Quinn, Susan. Marie Curie. *A Life*. New York: Simon and Schuster, 1995.

Didrickson Zaharias

Beatrice S. Smith. *The Babe: Mildred Didrickson Zaharias*. Milwaukee, Wisconsin: Raintree Publishers, 1976.

Knudson, R.R. *Babe Didrickson*. New York: Viking Penguin Inc., 1985.

Sanford, William R. *Babe Didrickson Zaharias*. New York: Macmillan Publishing Company, 1993.

Duncan

Duncan, Isadora. *My Life*. New York: W.W. Norton, 1927.

Kurth, Peter. *Isadora, a Sensational Life*. New York: Little Brown and Co. Inc., 2001.

Kozodoy, Ruth. *Isadora Duncan*. New York: Chelsea Publishers, 1988.

Seroff, Victor. *The Real Isadora*. New York: Dial Press, 1971.

Earhart

Morrel, Virginia. *Amelia Earhart*. Washington, D.C.: National Geographic, January 1999.

Lovell, Mary, S. *The Sound of Wings: The Life of Amelia Earhart*. New York: St. Martin's Press, 1989.

Morrisey, Muriel Earhart. *Amelia Earhart*. Santa Barbara, California: Bellerophon Books, 1992.

Moseley, Elizabeth. Amelia Earhart. New York: Chelsea House Publishers, 1991.

Keller

Keller, Helen. *The Story of My Life*. New York: Doubleday, 1954.

Lash, Joseph P. *Helen and Teacher. The Story of Helen Keller and Anne Sullivan Macy*. New York: Delacortes Press, 1980.

Wepman, Dennis. *Helen Keller*. Pennsylvania: Chelsea House Publishers
Broomall, 1987

Lindbergh

Lindbergh, Anne Morrow. *Gift from the Sea,* New York: Pantheon Books,
1975

Scott, Berg. *Lindbergh*. New York: The Berkeley Publishing Company, 1998.

*Locked Rooms and Open Doors: Diaries and Letters of Anne Morrow Lindbergh,
1933–1935.* A Helen and Kurt Wolff Book. San Diego: Harcourt, Inc,
1974. Copyright renewed by Jon M. Lindbergh, Reeve Lindbergh and
Land Morrow Lindbergh. 2003.

Meir

Meir, Golda. *My Life*. New York: G.P. Putnam's Sons, 1988.

Martin, Ralph G. *Golda Meir*: *The Romantic Years*. New York: Charles
Scribner's Sons, 1988.

Montgomery MacDonald

Gillen, Molly. *The Wheel of Things*. Markham, Ontario, Canada: Fitzhenry
and Whiteside Limited, 1978.

Montgomery, L.M. *The Alpine Path*. Don Mills, Ontario, Canada: Fitzhenry
and Whiteside Limited, 1975.

Montessori

Kramer, Rita. *Maria Montessori: A Biography*. New York: G.P. Putnam's Sons,
1976.

Waltuck, Margot R. *A Montessori Album*. Cleveland Heights, Ohio: Szavid
Kahn, 1986.

Standing, E.M. *Maria Montessori Her Life and Work*. New York: Penguin
Group, 1984.

Moses

Biracee,Tom. *Grandma Moses*. Broomall, Pennsylvania: Chelsea House Publishers, 1989.

Robertson, Mary Anna. *My Story*. New York: Harper and Row, Publishers, 1952.

Mother Teresa

Cunningham, Frank J. *Words to Love by*. Indiana: Ave Maria Press, 1988.

Mother Teresa, *No Greater Love*. Novato, California: New World Press, 2002.

Nightingale

Small, Hugh. *Florence Nightingale, Avenging Angel*. New York: St. Martin's Press, 1998.

Smith, Woodham. *Florence Nightingale*. New York: McGraw Hill, 1951.

O'Keeffe

Giboire, Clive (Editor) *Lovingly, Georgia: The Complete Correspondence of Georgia O'Keeffe and Anita Pollitzer*. New York: Simon and Schuster, 1990.

O'Keeffe, Georgia. *Georgia O'Keeffe*. New York: Viking Press, 1976.

Turner, Robyn Montana. *Georgia O'Keeffe, Portrait of Women Artists for Children*. Boston: Little, Brown and Company, 1991.

Peron

Evita Peron. Introduction by Joseph A. Page, *In My Own Words*. New York: The New Press, 1996.

Eva Peron. *La Razon de mi Vida (The Reason for my Life)*. Buenos Aires, Argentina: Peuser Editions, 1951.

Montgomery, Paul L. *Eva, Evita: The life and Death of Eva Peron,* New York: Pocket Books, a division of Simon and Schuster, 1979.

Roosevelt

Cook, Blanche Wiesen. *Eleanor Roosevelt*. New York: Penguin Books, 1993.

Lash, Joseph P. *Eleanor and Franklin*. New York: New American Library, 1973.

Queen Victoria

Cecil Woodham Smith, *Queen Victoria: From her birth to the death of the Prince Consort*. New York: Alfred A. Knopf, Inc. 1972.

Warner, Marina. *Queen Victoria's Sketchbook*. New York: Crown Publishers Inc., 1979.

Weintraub, Stanley. *Victoria: An Intimate Biography*. New York: E.P. Dutton, 1987.

Streatfield, Noel, *Queen Victoria*. New York: Random House, 1958.

GENERAL READING

American Women of Achievement, New York and Philadelphia: Chelsea House Publishing, 1989.

Bridgewater, William. *The Columbia Viking Desk Encyclopedia*. New York: Viking Press, 1968.

Research material, Buenos Aires, Argentina: The Eva Peron Historical Research Foundation, 2002.

Felder, Debora G. *The 100 Most Influential Women of All Time*. New York: Citadel Press, 1996.

Pope John Paul II. *Letter to Women of Fourth World Conference in Beijing*. Boston: St. Paul Books and Media, 1995.

Uglow, Jennifer S. *The Macmillan Dictionary of Women's Biography*. New York: The Continuum Publishing Company, 1998.

SELECTED READING

Allport, Gordon Willard and Vernon, Phillip E., *Studies in Expressive Movement*. New York: The Macmillan Co., 1933.

Baker, J. Newton Law LL.M., J.D. *Law of Disputed and Forged Documents*. Charlottesville, Virginia: The Ichie Company, 1955.

De Sainte Columbe, Paul, *Grapho-therapeutics*. Hollywood, California: Laurida Books Publishing Company, 1966.

Frankl, Viktor, E, *Man's Search For Meaning*. New York: Washington Square Press, 1946.

Green, Jane Nugent, *You and Your Private I*. Saint Paul, Minnesota: Lewellyn Publications, 1975.

Hall, Edward T, *The Silent Language*. Garden City, New York: Anchor Press/Double Day, 1973.

Harris, Thomas A., M.D., *I'm OK—You're O.K*. New York: Harper and Row, 1969.

Harrison, Wilson R. Ph.D., *Suspect Documents*. Chicago: Nelson Hall Publishing, 1981.

International Graphoanalysis Society Reference books:

Evaluation

Case Book No. 1

Case Book No. 2

Evaluated Traits

Effective Traits Description

Dictionary of Stroke Structures

The Encyclopedic Dictionary

Fears and Defenses

A Synopsis of Traits Volume 1 and 11

Journals 1955–2004

An Annotated Bibliography of Studies in Handwriting Analysis

Karohs, Erika *Encyclopedia for Handwriting Analysts*. Pebble Beach, California: Self-published, 1985.

Karohs, Erika *The Analysts Handbook*. Pebble Beach, California: Self-published, 1981.

Metzger, Mary, *Letters of the Alphabet Analyzed*. Oakdale, Pennsylvania: Analytical Handwriting Experts, 1981.

Osborne, Albert S. *Question Documents,* second edition, reprint. Chicago: Nelson-Hall, 1929.

Osborne, Albert S. *The Problem of Proof,* second edition. Chicago: Nelson-Hall, 1975.

Thornton, Tamara Plakins, *Handwriting in America*. New Haven and London: Yale University Press, 1996.

Yalon, Dafna editor, *Graphology Across Cultures*. Middlesex, England: The British Institute of Graphologists, 2003.

DICTIONARY
Definitions of stroke structures found within this book

The following definitions and illustrations are in accord with the findings of the International Graphoanalysis Society's research department. Handwriting is comprised of six elements; slant, depth, lines, circles, loops and hooks. These elements remain the same regardless of the language of the writer. In Graphoanalysis the true meaning of traits in large measure depends on their intensity, frequency, and interrelation with accompanying traits.

It should be noted that Graphoanalysis is unbiased. The race, age, or sex of the writer is not revealed. Additional information may be found at www.igas.com

ACQUISITIVENESS

An initial hook indicates acquisitiveness or the desire to obtain or possess. Large hooks indicate a desire for important possessions. Small hooks imply that the writer craves trivial things.

AGGRESSIVENESS

A stroke that swings out boldly from a downstroke points to aggressiveness. The writer pushes forward, strongly resisting anything or anyone that could obstruct a planned course of action.

ARGUMENTATIVE

p p p

If the first stroke of the letter *p* rises above the buckle of the letter *p*, the writer shows argumentativeness.

ARTISTIC INCLINATIONS

Monday   Sarah

Printed capital letters that begin a proper noun or a sentence reflect artistic inclinations.

ATTENTION, DESIRE FOR

a   d

Desire to attract attention is present if finals rise above the tops of a letter or word. When finals turn back, the writer has an excessive desire to be noticed; he or she will constantly find ways to be noticed.

BROAD-MINDEDNESS

broader

Well-rounded *e's* imply broad-mindedness, or tolerance of the views of others. This is also true of the *a, o, d, g, and q* circle formations. The writer can be tolerant of other opinions.

CAUTION

caution

When words end with a straight final stroke, usually at the end of a line, caution is indicated. The writer considers carefully before taking action.

CLANNISHNESS

g g

Small lower loops, often squared, which do not return to the baseline, point to clannishness, or extreme exclusiveness.

CONCENTRATION

Small writing suggests habitual concentration, or fixing one's attention on a single object or idea, to the exclusion of other influences. It intensifies all other traits in the personality.

CULTURAL DESIRES

prefer   raid

Greek *e*'s in writing manifest refinement of taste and manners. This Greek *e* formation may also appear in the letter *r*.

DECEPTION

cáll   cóuld

When a circle formation is double looped, there is an indication of deception.

DECISIVENESS

firm

When we see firm final strokes in writing, we may conclude that the writer is decisive. The writer has little difficulty making up his or her mind.

DEFIANCE

know   taKe

If the upper stroke of the letter *k* rises above the lower case letters, defiance is indicated. The writer may have a resistance to authority or opposition.

DELIBERATENESS

ft   in

Separated stems, slightly rounded at the top, imply that the writer will be deliberate in carrying out a task.

DETAILS, ATTENTION TO

Closely dotted *i*'s and *j*'s are evidence that the writer pays close attention to details; the closer the dot to the stem, the stronger the trait. People who pay close attention to details may also possess good memories.

DETERMINATION

Heavy downstrokes, descending below the baseline, with or without loops, give evidence of determination; the width or heaviness of the stroke indicates strength, whereas length indicates endurance. This is an indication of having resolve.

DIGNITY

If *d*- and *t*-stems are retraced or nearly retraced, dignity is implied. A high degree of worth, repute or honor is present.

DIPLOMACY

m̲ t̲ap̲er̲

When writing tapers in size toward the end of a letter formation, especially in the letter *m* or *n,* it indicates diplomacy. This can also be seen when the letters in a word taper. The writer is tactful in dealing with people.

DIRECTNESS

direct act

When letters begin with a simple, initial downstroke, directness is indicated. The writer goes to the heart of the matter.

DOMINATING

Strong t-bars, made with a forward and downward movement, frequently increasing in weight and ending decisively, are evidence of a dominating nature. The writer has the capacity to influence others through strength of will.

DOMINEERING NATURE

Strong *t*-bars that slant downward and taper to a point suggest a domineering nature, a tendency to impose one's opinion or ideas on others, even to the point of being sarcastic.

EGOTISM

Land   Rail

Very tall or large capitals are evidence of egotism; an inflated opinion of one's self.

EMOTIONAL DEPTH

light   heavy

Heaviness of the writing implies how deeply an emotional situation will affect the writer. A heavy-lined writer experiences life deeply. A light-lined writer recovers quickly from emotional experiences.

EMOTIONAL RESPONSE

head   heart   hidden
  a   b   c

Slant of writing determines emotional response, or how quickly a writer will respond to outside stimuli. In the examples above, (a) the head rules the feelings (b) the heart rules the feelings and (c) the feelings are hidden.

ENTHUSIASM

t

When a *t*-bar is long, enthusiasm is evident; the longer the bar, the greater the enthusiasm. The writer has a tendency to be eager and intense.

FLUIDITY

flag

Smooth-flowing strokes in connecting words or letter structures, such as in a *g* or *f*, point to the trait of fluidity, the capacity to make smooth transitions from one thought to another; the writer expresses him or herself easily in writing, speaking or acting.

FRANKNESS

am out

If a circle formation has no hooks or loops, frankness is indicated.

GENEROSITY

yes

When a final stroke is extended to at least the width of the preceding letter, before turning upward, the writer shows generosity. The writer will have a willingness to give or share.

GOALS

To To to to to
 a   b   c   d   e

The strokes that form the letter *t* are among the most important of the alphabetical structures. The above examples illustrate the location of the *t*-bars and where the writer places his goals in life. (a) visionary (b) distant (c) high (d) practical, and (e) low. Goals indicate the end the writer wishes to attain.

HUMOR

If the beginning stroke begins with a graceful flourish, which flows smoothly into the following downstroke, a sense of humor is indicated. The writer may have the ability to see or express that which is funny or amusing.

IMAGINATION, ABSTRACT

Upper loop letters indicate abstract imagination. The imagination could be at a theoretical, philosophical, or religious level; the larger the loop, the more active the imagination.

IMAGINATION, MATERIAL

The occurrence of loops below the baseline point to the presence of imagination in the everyday world; the more inflated the loop, the greater the imagination.

INDECISIVENESS

Feathered or tapered finals suggest indecisiveness. The writer can show hesitation or difficulty in making up his or her mind.

INDEPENDENT THINKING

When *d-* and *t-*stems are short in relation to the height of the lower case letters, there is evidence of independence. The writer is not bound by custom; he or she will act on his own conclusions.

INITIATIVE

When strokes above the baseline leap forward sharply from the preceding downstroke, such as in the letter *h*, the writer may show initiative or the ability to act, when opportunity presents itself.

INTUITION

Frequent breaks between cursive letters are evidence of intuition. It is assumed that the writer has the power to grasp knowledge without rational thought or inference.

IRRITABILITY

i j

Jabbed *i-* and *j*-dots suggest irritability. The writer has the potential to be impatient or easily annoyed.

JEALOUSY

m You

The stroke indicating jealousy is a clockwise initial loop that is flattened or *ovalled* to at least some degree. It occurs at the beginning of a letter structure and it must be closed. The writer can show fear of rivalry.

LOYALTY

i j

Loyalty is shown when *i*-and *j*-dots are round and firm. The writer is loyal to what he or she believes is right.

OPTIMISM

t up

Up-slanted *t*-bars, up-turned finals, or writing that has an inclined baseline, indicate that optimism is present. The writer will tend to be hopeful, looking on the bright side of life.

ORGANIZATIONAL ABILITY

food

If the upper and lower loops are balanced, often seen in the letter *f,* we may conclude that the writer has organizational ability. The writer has the capacity for systematic planning and arrangement of objects, ideas or tasks.

PERSISTENCE

f f

Tied strokes in *f*'s and other letters imply that persistence is present. The writer will keep trying after setbacks.

PRIDE

do to

Tall *d*- and t-stems, 2 to 2 1 / 2 times the height of the lower case letters, give evidence of pride. Normally the stems are retraced, but pride is also seen in looped form. Pride is an asset when it motivates high standards in work, appearance and behavior.

PROCRASTINATION

i j t

When *i*-dots or *t*-crossings appear to the left of the stem, one may conclude that the writer procrastinates or puts off until tomorrow what should be done today.

RESENTMENT

resentment

A straight initial stroke that starts at or below the baseline of a letter implies resentment, or alertness to imposition. The further below the baseline the stroke begins, the stronger the trait.

RESPONSIBILITY, DESIRE FOR

Many

Large initial clockwise loops, particularly on capital letter structures, give evidence that the writer has a desire for responsibility and is willing to accept additional duties. The loop must be closed.

RHYTHM

rhythm

The regular return of the writing to the baseline, or writing that has a "beat," suggests that the individual possesses the quality of rhythm. The writer will think and move in an orderly manner. Careful spacing of letters also contributes to rhythm.

SARCASM

Arrow-like t-bars indicate sarcasm. The shorter the bar and the sharper the point, the more painful is the sarcasm.

SECRETIVENESS

A circle structure closed with loop indicates secretiveness, a tendency to conceal one's thoughts, feelings or affairs.

SELF-CASTIGATION

Back-lashed *t*-bars mean self-castigation. This is a tendency to blame one's self for circumstances that are beyond his or her control.

SELF-CONFIDENCE

Good sized capital letters indicate good to strong confidence in one's self. (It should be noted that the position of the *t*-bar on the *t*-stem also defines self-confidence).

SELF-CONSCIOUSNESS

When the last structure of the letter *m* or *n* is taller than the preceding struc-ture, the writer is self-conscious. This can also be seen in the double *l*. The writer is shy or ill at ease when placed in unfamiliar situations.

SELF-CONTROL

A cross-bar on the letter *t,* bent into a dome-like bow, implies a bending of the will. This trait suggests that the writer is trying to overcome a habit or create a new one.

SELF-DECEIT

A loop to the left of a circle structure offers evidence of self-deceit. The writer will not be honest about certain areas of his or her life.

SELF-RELIANCE

Underscored names indicate self-reliance. The writer will wants to accom-plish his aims without help from others.

SENSITIVENESS TO CRITICISM

Looped *d* and *t* formations suggest that the writer is sensitive to criticism or easily offended. It can be imagined or real. The more inflated the loop, the greater the sensitivity.

SHALLOWNESS

When the cross-bar of the *t* resembles a basin, shallowness of purpose is indicated. The writer takes a light attitude toward goals or purposes.

SHOWMANSHIP

Over-sized, flowing or ornamental writing especially in capitals, displays the desire to be noticed. When done with taste and simplicity, it indicates showmanship.

SLANT: (see emotional responsiveness)

SPACE
Space, in handwriting, refers to the frequency with which spaces appear between letters and words; the greater the space, the more the writer needs his or her privacy.

STUBBORNESS

A tent-like formation, more often noted in a *d* or *t,* suggests that the writer is stubborn; she will not give in.

TALKATIVE

Open-topped letter formations indicate talkativeness, a desire to communicate orally. (It should be noted that talkativeness may be present *without* open-topped letter formation; such writers chatter on without revealing what they are really thinking).

TEMPER

A relatively heavy t-bar to the right of the stem, indicates temper. The writer has a tendency to feel anger easily.

TENACITY

A final hook points to tenacity. It is the quality of holding fast to what one has; possessions, people, or abstract ideas.

THINKING, ANALYTICAL

My My

When *v*-shaped wedges come down to the baseline, the writer shows analytical ability. The sharper the wedges, the more penetrating the writer's ability to analyze.

THINKING, LOGICAL

More

Rounded *m's* and *n's,* often accompanied by flat-topped *r's,* point to cumulative or logical thinking. The writer accumulates facts before arriving at a decision.

THINKING, QUICK

many

Needle-like retracing of *m's*, *n's* or *h's* indicates an instant grasp of subjects with which the writer is familiar.

UNYIELDING:

so

When the letter formation is firm, as in the letter *s* with a point, the writer is unyielding. The writer will not be susceptible to influence, or be easily swayed.

VANITY

If the *d*-and *t*-stems are excessively tall, vanity is indicated, an exaggerated high opinion of one's ability, appearance and possessions.

WILL POWER

A relatively heavy *t*-bar is evidence of a strong will power. When the cross-bar is long, enthusiasm is added.

WORRY

Many

When the down stroke of an *m* or *n* makes a loop on its return, there is an indication of unrealistic imagination. This implies worry or even anguish. It often appears in capital letters.

YIELDINGNESS

so

A soft or rounded letter structure, particularly an *s,* implies a yielding nature. The writer is susceptible to influence.